TILL WE HAVE FACES:
A MYTH RETOLD

A Reading Companion

Christine L. Norvell
an any day companion for an everyday reader

Copyright © 2017 Christine L. Norvell
TILL WE HAVE FACES: A MYTH RETOLD – A Reading Companion
By Christine L. Norvell

ISBN-13: 978-1544680880
ISBN-10: 1544680880

All rights reserved.

No part of this book may be used or reproduced by any means, graphic, electronic, or mechanical, including photocopying, recording, taping or by any information storage retrieval system without the written permission of the author except in the case of brief quotations embodied in critical articles and reviews.

Unless otherwise noted, scripture taken from the Holy Bible, English Standard Version Copyright © 2001 by Crossway, from the Complete Jewish Bible ® Copyright © 1998 by David H. Stern, Lederer Messianic Publications.

Cover illustration by Dan Rempel at DanRempelIllustration.com.

Table of Contents

Introduction xi

PART I 1

    Chapter 1 .... *3*
    Chapter 2 .... *7*
    Chapter 3 .... *11*
    Chapter 4 .... *14*
    Chapter 5 .... *17*
    Chapter 6 .... *21*
    Chapter 7 .... *24*
    Chapter 8 .... *28*
    Chapter 9 .... *31*
    Chapter 10 .... *35*
    Chapter 11 .... *38*
    Chapter 12 .... *40*
    Chapter 13 .... *43*
    Chapter 14 .... *46*
    Chapter 15 .... *50*
    Chapter 16 .... *53*
    Chapter 17 .... *57*
    Chapter 18 .... *60*
    Chapter 19 .... *63*
    Chapter 20 .... *66*
    Chapter 21 .... *69*

PART II 73

    Chapter 1 .... *75*
    Chapter 2 .... *78*
    Chapter 3 .... *82*
    Chapter 4 .... *87*

Conclusion 92

About the Author 97

To my most precious family of five, my praying parents,
and the flames of blue that surround this world (Isaiah 10:16-17).

To my heavenly Father, my Papa, for loving me wholly,
for listening to me, for speaking to me in daily bread portions.

ACKNOWLEDGMENTS

With gratitude to the scholars and thinkers who have gone before me, most especially Peter J. Schakel for his spiritual and academic insights that shaped my thoughts and my classroom discussions.

Without the laboratory of the classroom, my studies, thoughts, and questions would be incomplete. Thank you to Regent Preparatory School for preparing me to write.

"To construct plausible and moving 'other worlds' you must draw on the only real 'other world' we know, that of the spirit." —C.S. Lewis, "On Stories"

Introduction

*I will incline my ear and consent to a
proverb; On the harp, I will unfold my riddle.*
—Psalm 49:4 (Amp)

HAVING TAUGHT THE novel for a decade, I'm still surprised when C. S. Lewis fans mention to me that they don't get the story. More than once, I've heard "How could this be Lewis's favorite? Why?" Or "I like the first part of the story, but the second part is so ambiguous." Or how about "Are you sure this was his last novel?" I could present an academic analysis to satisfy those questions and join troops of others culling opinions and research. Yet that is not my intent. My desire is to be your companion as we read together in our own one-on-one book club if you will. Part summary, part commentary, and a touch of analysis. My hope is that this companion guide will not only deepen your understanding of Lewis's hope, but that it will also deepen your own view of redemption.

In preparation for the novel, take a few minutes to read the original Greek myth, "Cupid and Psyche." Lewis himself was partial to one of the earliest Greek versions from the second century by Apuleius, who Lewis credits as a source but not as a model for his story. I enjoy a longer, more storied version, as do my students, such as Thomas Bulfinch's narrative in *The Age of Fable*.

CUPID AND PSYCHE[1]

A CERTAIN KING and queen had three daughters. The charms of the two elder were more than common, but the beauty of the youngest was so wonderful that the poverty of language is unable to express its due praise. The fame of her beauty was so great that strangers from neighboring countries came in crowds to enjoy the sight, and looked on her with amazement, paying her that homage which is due only to Venus herself. In fact Venus found her altars deserted, while men turned their devotion to this young virgin. As she passed along, the people sang her praises, and strewed her way with chaplets and flowers.

This perversion of homage due only to the immortal powers to the exaltation of a mortal gave great offence to the real Venus. Shaking her ambrosial locks with indignation, she exclaimed, "Am I then to be eclipsed in my honors by a mortal girl? In vain then did that royal shepherd, whose judgment was approved by Jove himself, give me the palm of beauty over my illustrious rivals, Pallas and Juno. But she shall not so quietly usurp my honors. I will give her cause to repent of so unlawful a beauty."

Thereupon she calls her winged son Cupid, mischievous enough in his own nature, and rouses and provokes him yet more by her complaints. She points out Psyche to him and says, "My dear son, punish that contumacious beauty; give thy mother a revenge as sweet as her injuries are great; infuse into the bosom of that haughty girl a passion for some low, mean, unworthy being, so that she may reap a mortification as great as her present exultation and triumph."

Cupid prepared to obey the commands of his mother. There are two fountains in Venus's garden, one of sweet waters, the other of bitter. Cupid filled two amber vases, one from each

---

[1] Bulfinch, Thomas. *The Age of Fable.* New York: Review of Reviews, 1913; Bartleby.com, 2000. www.bartleby.com/bulfinch/. © 2000 Copyright Bartleby.com, Inc.

fountain, and suspending them from the top of his quiver, hastened to the chamber of Psyche, whom he found asleep. He shed a few drops from the bitter fountain over her lips, though the sight of her almost moved him to pity; then touched her side with the point of his arrow. At the touch she awoke, and opened eyes upon Cupid (himself invisible), which so startled him that in his confusion he wounded himself with his own arrow. Heedless of his wound, his whole thought now was to repair the mischief he had done, and he poured the balmy drops of joy over all her silken ringlets.

Psyche, henceforth frowned upon by Venus, derived no benefit from all her charms. True, all eyes were cast eagerly upon her, and every mouth spoke her praises; but neither king, royal youth, nor plebeian presented himself to demand her in marriage. Her two elder sisters of moderate charms had now long been married to two royal princes; but Psyche, in her lonely apartment, deplored her solitude, sick of that beauty which, while it procured abundance of flattery, had failed to awaken love.

Her parents, afraid that they had unwittingly incurred the anger of the gods, consulted the oracle of Apollo, and received this answer: "The virgin is destined for the bride of no mortal lover. Her future husband awaits her on the top of the mountain. He is a monster whom neither gods nor men can resist."

This dreadful decree of the oracle filled all the people with dismay, and her parents abandoned themselves to grief. But Psyche said, "Why, my dear parents, do you now lament me? You should rather have grieved when the people showered upon me undeserved honors, and with one voice called me a Venus. I now perceive that I am a victim to that name. I submit. Lead me to that rock to which my unhappy fate has destined me." Accordingly, all things being prepared, the royal maid took her place in the procession, which more resembled a funeral than a nuptial pomp, and with her parents, amid the lamentations of the people, ascended the mountain, on the summit of which they left her alone, and with sorrowful hearts returned home.

While Psyche stood on the ridge of the mountain, panting with fear and with eyes full of tears, the gentle Zephyr raised her from the earth and bore her with an easy motion into a flowery dale. By degrees her mind became composed, and she laid herself down on the grassy bank to sleep. When she awoke refreshed with sleep, she looked round and beheld near by a pleasant grove of tall and stately trees. She entered it, and in the midst discovered a fountain, sending forth clear and crystal waters, and fast by, a magnificent palace whose august front impressed the spectator that it was not the work of mortal hands, but the happy retreat of some god. Drawn by admiration and wonder, she approached the building and ventured to enter. Every object she met filled her with pleasure and amazement. Golden pillars supported the vaulted roof, and the walls were enriched with carvings and paintings representing beasts of the chase and rural scenes, adapted to delight the eye of the beholder. Proceeding onward, she perceived that besides the apartments of state there were others filled with all manner of treasures, and beautiful and precious productions of nature and art.

While her eyes were thus occupied, a voice addressed her, though she saw no one, uttering these words: "Sovereign lady, all that you see is yours. We whose voices you hear are your servants and shall obey all your commands with our utmost care and diligence. Retire, therefore, to your chamber and repose on your bed of down, and when you see fit repair to the bath. Supper awaits you in the adjoining alcove when it pleases you to take your seat there."

Psyche gave ear to the admonitions of her vocal attendants, and after repose and the refreshment of the bath, seated herself in the alcove, where a table immediately presented itself, without any visible aid from waiters or servants, and covered with the greatest delicacies of food and the most nectareous wines. Her ears too were feasted with music from invisible performers; of whom one sang, another played on the lute, and all closed in the wonderful harmony of a full chorus.

She had not yet seen her destined husband. He came only in the hours of darkness and fled before the dawn of morning, but his accents were full of love, and inspired a like passion in her. She often begged him to stay and let her behold him, but he would not consent. On the contrary he charged her to make no attempt to see him, for it was his pleasure, for the best of reasons, to keep concealed. "Why should you wish to behold me?" he said; "have you any doubt of my love? have you any wish ungratified? If you saw me, perhaps you would fear me, perhaps adore me, but all I ask of you is to love me. I would rather you would love me as an equal than adore me as a god."

This reasoning somewhat quieted Psyche for a time, and while the novelty lasted she felt quite happy. But at length the thought of her parents, left in ignorance of her fate, and of her sisters, precluded from sharing with her the delights of her situation, preyed on her mind and made her begin to feel her palace as but a splendid prison. When her husband came one night, she told him her distress, and at last drew from him an unwilling consent that her sisters should be brought to see her.

So, calling Zephyr, she acquainted him with her husband's commands, and he, promptly obedient, soon brought them across the mountain down to their sister's valley. They embraced her and she returned their caresses. "Come," said Psyche, "enter with me my house and refresh yourselves with whatever your sister has to offer." Then taking their hands she led them into her golden palace, and committed them to the care of her numerous train of attendant voices, to refresh them in her baths and at her table, and to show them all her treasures. The view of these celestial delights caused envy to enter their bosoms, at seeing their young sister possessed of such state and splendor, so much exceeding their own.

They asked her numberless questions, among others what sort of a person her husband was. Psyche replied that he was a beautiful youth, who generally spent the daytime in hunting upon the mountains. The sisters, not satisfied with this reply, soon made her confess that she had never seen him. Then they proceeded to fill her bosom with dark suspicions. "Call to mind," they said, "the Pythian oracle that declared you destined to marry a direful and tremendous monster. The inhabitants of this valley say that your husband is a terrible and monstrous serpent, who nourishes you for a while with dainties that he may by and by devour you. Take our advice. Provide yourself with a lamp and a sharp knife; put them in concealment that your husband may not discover them, and when he is sound asleep, slip out of bed, bring forth your lamp, and see for yourself whether what they say is true or not. If it is, hesitate not to cut off the monster's head, and thereby recover your liberty."

Psyche resisted these persuasions as well as she could, but they did not fail to have their effect on her mind, and when her sisters were gone, their words and her own curiosity were too strong for her to resist. So she prepared her lamp and a sharp knife, and hid them out of sight of her husband. When he had fallen into his first sleep, she silently rose and uncovering her lamp beheld not a hideous monster, but the most beautiful and charming of the gods, with his golden ringlets wandering over his snowy neck and crimson cheek, with two dewy wings on his shoulders, whiter than snow, and with shining feathers like the tender blossoms of spring. As she leaned the lamp over to have a nearer view of his face a drop of burning oil fell on the shoulder of the god, startled with which he opened his eyes and fixed them full upon her; then, without saying one word, he spread his white wings and flew out of the window. Psyche, in vain endeavoring to follow him, fell from the window to the ground. Cupid, beholding her as she lay in the dust, stopped his flight for an instant and said, "O foolish Psyche, is it thus you repay my love? After having disobeyed my mother's commands and made you my wife, will you think me a monster and cut off my head? But go; return to your sisters, whose advice you seem to think preferable to mine. I inflict no other punishment on you than to leave you forever. Love cannot dwell with suspicion." So saying, he fled away, leaving poor

Psyche prostrate on the ground, filling the place with mournful lamentations.

When she had recovered some degree of composure she looked around her, but the palace and gardens had vanished, and she found herself in the open field not far from the city where her sisters dwelt. She repaired thither and told them the whole story of her misfortunes, at which, pretending to grieve, those spiteful creatures inwardly rejoiced. "For now," said they, "he will perhaps choose one of us." With this idea, without saying a word of her intentions, each of them rose early the next morning and ascended the mountains, and having reached the top, called upon Zephyr to receive her and bear her to his lord; then leaping up, and not being sustained by Zephyr, fell down the precipice and was dashed to pieces.

Psyche meanwhile wandered day and night, without food or repose, in search of her husband. Casting her eyes on a lofty mountain having on its brow a magnificent temple, she sighed and said to herself, "Perhaps my love, my lord, inhabits there," and directed her steps thither.

She had no sooner entered than she saw heaps of corn, some in loose ears and some in sheaves, with mingled ears of barley. Scattered about, lay sickles and rakes, and all the instruments of harvest, without order, as if thrown carelessly out of the weary reapers' hands in the sultry hours of the day.

This unseemly confusion the pious Psyche put an end to, by separating and sorting everything to its proper place and kind, believing that she ought to neglect none of the gods, but endeavor by her piety to engage them all in her behalf. The holy Ceres, whose temple it was, finding her so religiously employed, thus spoke to her: "O Psyche, truly worthy of our pity, though I cannot shield you from the frowns of Venus, yet I can teach you how best to allay her displeasure. Go, then, and voluntarily surrender yourself to your lady and sovereign, and try by modesty and submission to win her forgiveness, and perhaps her favor will restore you the husband you have lost."

Psyche obeyed the commands of Ceres and took her way to the temple of Venus, endeavoring to fortify her mind and ruminating on what she should say and how best propitiate the angry goddess, feeling that the issue was doubtful and perhaps fatal.

Venus received her with angry countenance. "Most undutiful and faithless of servants," said she, "do you at last remember that you really have a mistress? Or have you rather come to see your sick husband, yet laid up of the wound given him by his loving wife? You are so ill-favored and disagreeable that the only way you can merit your lover must be by dint of industry and diligence. I will make trial of your housewifery." Then she ordered Psyche to be led to the storehouse of her temple, where was laid up a great quantity of wheat, barley, millet, vetches, beans, and lentils prepared for food for her pigeons, and said, "Take and separate all these grains, putting all of the same kind in a parcel by themselves, and see that you get it done before evening." Then Venus departed and left her to her task.

But Psyche, in a perfect consternation at the enormous work, sat stupid and silent, without moving a finger to the inextricable heap.

While she sat despairing, Cupid stirred up the little ant, a native of the fields, to take compassion on her. The leader of the ant hill, followed by whole hosts of his six-legged subjects, approached the heap, and with the utmost diligence, taking grain by grain, they separated the pile, sorting each kind to its parcel; and when it was all done, they vanished out of sight in a moment.

Venus at the approach of twilight returned from the banquet of the gods, breathing odors and crowned with roses. Seeing the task done, she exclaimed, "This is no work of yours, wicked one, but his, whom to your own and his misfortune you have enticed." So saying, she threw her a piece of black bread for her supper and went away.

Next morning Venus ordered Psyche to be called and said to her, "Behold yonder grove which stretches along the margin of the water. There you will find sheep feeding without a shepherd, with golden-shining fleeces on their backs. Go, fetch me a sample of that precious wool gathered from every one of their fleeces."

Psyche obediently went to the riverside, prepared to do her best to execute the command. But the river god inspired the reeds with harmonious murmurs, which seemed to say, "O maiden, severely tried, tempt not the dangerous flood, nor venture among the formidable rams on the other side, for as long as they are under the influence of the rising sun, they burn with a cruel rage to destroy mortals with their sharp horns or rude teeth. But when the noontide sun has driven the cattle to the shade, and the serene spirit of the flood has lulled them to rest, you may then cross in safety, and you will find the woolly gold sticking to the bushes and the trunks of the trees."

Thus the compassionate river god gave Psyche instructions how to accomplish her task, and by observing his directions she soon returned to Venus with her arms full of the golden fleece; but she received not the approbation of her implacable mistress, who said, "I know very well it is by none of your own doings that you have succeeded in this task, and I am not satisfied yet that you have any capacity to make yourself useful. But I have another task for you. Here, take this box and go your way to the infernal shades, and give this box to Proserpine and say, 'My mistress Venus desires you to send her a little of your beauty, for in tending her sick son she has lost some of her own.' Be not too long on your errand, for I must paint myself with it to appear at the circle of the gods and goddesses this evening."

Psyche was now satisfied that her destruction was at hand, being obliged to go with her own feet directly down to Erebus. Wherefore, to make no delay of what was not to be avoided, she goes to the top of a high tower to precipitate herself headlong, thus to descend the shortest way to the shades below. But a voice from the tower said to her, "Why, poor unlucky girl, dost thou design to put an end to thy days in so dreadful a manner? And what cowardice makes thee sink under this last danger who hast been so miraculously supported in all thy former?" Then the voice told her how by a certain cave she might reach the realms of Pluto, and how to avoid all the dangers of the road, to pass by Cerberus, the three-headed dog, and prevail on Charon, the ferryman, to take her across the black river and bring her back again. But the voice added, "When Proserpine has given you the box filled with her beauty, of all things this is chiefly to be observed by you, that you never once open or look into the box nor allow your curiosity to pry into the treasure of the beauty of the goddesses."

Psyche, encouraged by this advice, obeyed it in all things, and taking heed to her ways travelled safely to the kingdom of Pluto. She was admitted to the palace of Proserpine, and without accepting the delicate seat or delicious banquet that was offered her, but contented with coarse bread for her food, she delivered her message from Venus. Presently the box was returned to her, shut and filled with the precious commodity. Then she returned the way she came, and glad was she to come out once more into the light of day.

But having got so far successfully through her dangerous task, a longing desire seized her to examine the contents of the box. "What," said she, "shall I, the carrier of this divine beauty, not take the least bit to put on my cheeks to appear to more advantage in the eyes of my beloved husband!" So she carefully opened the box, but found nothing there of any beauty at all, but an infernal and truly Stygian sleep, which being thus set free from its prison, took possession of her, and she fell down in the midst of the road, a sleepy corpse without sense or motion.

Cupid, being now recovered from his wound, and not able longer to bear the absence of his beloved Psyche, slipping through the smallest crack of the window of his chamber which happened to be left open, flew to the spot where Psyche lay, and gathering up the sleep from her body closed it again in the box, and waked Psyche with a light touch of one of his arrows. "Again," said he, "hast thou almost perished by the same curiosity. But now perform exactly the task imposed on you by my mother, and I will take care of the rest."

Then Cupid, as swift as lightning penetrating the heights of heaven, presented himself before Jupiter with his supplication. Jupiter lent a favoring ear, and pleaded the cause of the lovers so earnestly with Venus that he won her consent. On this he sent Mercury to bring Psyche up to the heavenly assembly, and when she arrived, handing her a cup of ambrosia, he said, "Drink this, Psyche, and be immortal; nor shall Cupid ever break away from the knot in which he is tied, but these nuptials shall be perpetual."

Thus Psyche became at last united to Cupid, and in due time they had a daughter born to them whose name was Pleasure.

PART I

As you begin Lewis's tale, use each chapter commentary
either as a preface or a reflection to aid your reading.

Chapter 1
A PARTIAL MEMOIR

*"that was the first time I
clearly understood that I am ugly"*

OUR CENTRAL CHARACTER Orual begins in retrospective, almost bemoaning the end of her life and yet determined to tell us of her youth. As she clarifies that the gods can do nothing to her now, Orual also accuses them, making her "complaint," especially against the god of the Grey Mountain, Ungit's son. We quickly understand that Ungit is indeed Lewis' form for Venus from the original myth. A shapeless black mound in a smoky, dark temple, Ungit and her priest are described as Orual's first cemented fears. According to Orual, Ungit both hates Orual and is terrible in strength, for she requires sacrifice and bloodshed.

Though we aren't given a specific time period, we do know that the ancient country of Glome exists at the time of the Greeklands. Its barbarism and pagan culture are clear.

Let's carefully consider each character as they are introduced in this chapter. Orual is a decrepit old queen at story's beginning, but as narrator, she bluntly states that as the oldest daughter of King Trom, she is different as we see with her hair being "shorn" or shaved off—"the first time I clearly understood that I am ugly" (11).[2] As an old woman, she simply states that she *is* ugly, not that she *was,* as the reader would expect.

Ungit resides in her temple alone in the darkness with

---

[2] All quotations from Lewis are from *Till We Have Faces* (New York: Harcourt Brace, 1980) and are documented by page number in the text.

nothing but a smoke hole for light in the ceiling. Orual firmly and simply states that "She is a black stone without head or hands or face, and a strong goddess" (4). As a child, Orual describes "the girls who are kept in her house, and the presents the brides have to make to her, and how we sometimes, in a bad year, have to cut someone's throat and pour the blood over her" (7). Orual's tutor, the Fox, equates Ungit with the Greek goddess Aphrodite. The Fox specifically tells the story of how Aphrodite seduces the prince Anchises, tricking him into thinking she was mortal.

Anchises awakens from their bed of love, fully aware that he had been duped into sleeping with an immortal (8). As a child, Orual felt this tricksy behavior was typical of Aphrodite or Ungit. In Greek legend according to Hesiod, Aphrodite was born when Uranus, the father of the gods, was castrated by his son Cronus. Cronus threw the severed genitals into the ocean which began to churn and foam about them. From the *aphros* or "sea foam" arose Aphrodite, and the sea carried her to either Cyprus or Cythera. Hence she is often referred to as Kypris and Cytherea. Homer calls her a daughter of Zeus and Dione.[3] After her birth, Zeus was afraid that the gods would fight over Aphrodite's hand in marriage so he married her off to the smith god Hephaestus, the steadiest of the gods. He could hardly believe his good luck and used all his skills to make the most lavish jewels for her.

Hephaestus made her a girdle of finely wrought gold and wove magic into the filigree work. That was not very wise of him, for when she wore her magic girdle no one could resist her, and she was all too irresistible already. She loved gaiety and glamour and was not at all pleased at being the wife of sooty, hard-working Hephaestus.[4] This is Aphrodite, this is Ungit, and she is most temperamental.

---

[3] "Aphrodite." *Encyclopedia Mythica*. 2015. Encyclopedia Mythica Online. http://www.pantheon.org/articles/a/aphrodite.html.
[4] Ibid.

Redival is Orual's younger sister, a natural beauty with golden curls (5). She dislikes studying and teases and torments the Fox (9). That she instigates pranks against the Fox is no surprise.

As nursemaid and slave, Batta is "a big-boned, fair-haired, hard-handed woman" purchased from traders (5). My students often think she has callused hands, but her cruel nature implies that she hits and slaps to discipline Orual and Redival. She rants and threatens the girls with the idea of an impending stepmother. Batta is ever the evil caretaker herself, who delights in using pain to control others (6), very much like an enforcer or mob boss.

Hired to instruct a future prince, the Fox, a fellow slave, is from the Greeklands. He is "short and thick-set... He was very bright-eyed, and whatever of his hair and beard was not grey was reddish" (6). Orual delights in describing him as inquisitive and happy regardless of his slave status. She loved him "better than anyone I had yet known" (7). The Fox is a skilled tutor who enjoys the beauty of poetry yet regularly proclaims to Orual that such stories are "lies of poets" (8). Yet poetry, perhaps the fanciful and imaginative, is itself a reward for Orual's diligent work in all subjects.

Trom of Glome is practically Batta's mirror image. Often demanding, sometimes raging, he knows nothing of kindness, fatherhood, or leadership. Our first insight is his intentional cruelty to Orual when Trom says perhaps the Fox "can make her wise; it's about all she'll ever be good for" (7). Trom reveals to his daughters that he has made a match for himself to the *third* daughter of Caphad. I always wonder why Trom makes this proud announcement. How is the third princess an advantage? Was Lewis simply trying to show us Trom's ignorance, his ineptitude? Nevertheless the marriage moves forward, and King Trom demands that his daughters and others perform a Greek hymn under the Fox's tutelage at his wedding.

The Priest of Ungit is scarcely mentioned in this first chapter, but we do see his effect upon Orual. Inspiring fear, he smelled of animal and human sacrifice (11), wine, and incense, something Orual comes to call "the Ungit smell" (11). His bird mask and the animal skins clothing him present a terrifying figure. The Priest is the one who first mentions the idea of veils at the wedding. Trom heartily agrees because he doesn't want his innocent bride to take fright at the ugliness of Orual. Again, the Priest insists on the veils first, that tangible separation and covering. We soon realize that this is a significant theme for Lewis.

Unnamed, the third daughter of Caphad is not to be feared as a stereotypical stepmother. Orual describes her as tiny, beautiful, and most importantly, of little consequence. Most notably, she is pictured as "thickly veiled" as Orual (12). Why? Is her beauty to be covered equally as Orual's ugliness? The new stepmother is equally full of fear of the King as Orual is. Beauty is no protection against fear.

At chapter's end, Lewis noticeably refrains from introducing Psyche, the central character of the original myth.

Chapter 2
DEATH AND BIRTH

*"in one hour, I passed out of the worst anguish
I had yet suffered into the beginning of all my joys"*

ORUAL CARES FOR her stepmother "more like a sister" (14). Soon pregnant, the new Queen is homesick and lonely, not a figure to be feared. In fact, she quickly admits to Orual that she was afraid of her at first. The King is predictably delighted with the pregnancy, boasting about the prince to be born and making faithful sacrifices to Ungit.

Barbarism and superstition abound. All stay awake as the king and queen's child comes into the world or else the child might "refuse to wake in the world" (14). So too all doors must be kept open, for "the shutting of a door might shut up the mother's womb" (14). Lewis' imagery is both horrific and vital here. He combines the impressions of young Orual with the terrible demands of Ungit amidst a scene of red. From red flaring torches to the suggestion of a womb to the great fire to the spilled blood on the floor, all Orual sees is nightmarish and fearful, for Ungit requires sacrifice.

Even more startling is the King's departure from his dead Queen's room. Orual says he was not in his "red rage" but a pale one, "when he was pale, he was deadly" (15).

As an audience, we are not surprised by the King's reaction. Temperamental as ever, the King is livid with Ungit, and in a literal blind rage, he stabs the slave boy clad in white who dared to bring him wine. More blood is spilled.

The greatest of ironies is that this young boy was likely one of the many bastard sons in the palace that we hear of later. Poor

Trom. He can sire a boy in any illicit relationship, just not a royal one.

In a typical fit, he confronts the Priest, demanding justice of Ungit. The Priest is immovable and threatens Trom with Ungit's judgment while Trom explodes, raving against a plague of girls, lifting Orual by the hair and throwing her across the room. In his rage, Trom yells that the Fox will go to the mines and at one point yells, "Faces, faces, faces," as the rest stare at him. Of course we notice the reference to Lewis' title, but what does he really see?

Orual, and even the Fox, are filled with fear at their separation, but it was not to be. A contingent of men from the neighboring country of Phars arrives, and the Fox's help is needed. No thought of the mines or the King's sentence now. Though it annoys Orual and takes the Fox from her, the King has come to rely on the Fox for reading, calculating, and negotiations. He is ever the wise advisor to the King's ignorant bluster.

From the beginning of this chapter, the Fox has become a father figure for Orual; she calls him "grandfather," and he calls her "daughter." Orual's small world is black and white. Her father the King is an abuser and tyrant while the Fox, a slave no less, is caring and instructive. Orual calls him "a true grandfather now" with the birth of Psyche (21).

One more sacrifice perpetuates the images of slaughter—the King burns the dead queen's body (20), and she is no longer mentioned.

Imagery surrounding the infant Psyche is a direct contrast. She is large and healthy unlike her mother, "very fair of skin" (20) and quiet unlike her father. Formally named Istra, she comes to be known by the Greek version Psyche.

Even the Fox compares her to Helen of Troy (21) and says she is as beautiful as a goddess. She brought immediate joy to Orual— "I laughed because she was always laughing" (21).

Here, I'm reminded of Lewis's words in his autobiography *Surprised by Joy*. Joy is not derived from pleasure, "but even from aesthetic pleasure.

It must have the stab, the pang, the inconsolable longing."[5] It is both a simple delight and an unquenchable longing at the same time. For Lewis, the mention of joy implies a spiritual need within us, and of course, for Orual.

Psyche was a natural beauty "at every age the beauty proper to that age" and "she made beauty all around her" (22). One other distinctive contrast is Redival's natural beauty. Here, she is developing as a young woman but her beauty isn't unique. And if Redival is coming of age, then Orual must already be that much older. For Orual, creation itself is more beautiful in every season because of Psyche's presence.

And now time quickens for Orual. Seasons pass as Psyche matures. Perhaps one of Orual's most revealing passages yet is when she expresses Psyche's effect upon her:

> I wanted to be a wife so that I could have been her real mother. I wanted to be a boy so that she could be in love with me. I wanted her to be my full sister instead of my half sister. I wanted her to be a slave so that I could set her free and make her rich (23).

Her comments are striking, even awkward for us to read. We know she isn't being literal, but why so selfish? Does Orual want to rule or control Psyche? The pressing question might be whether this is an absolute unconditional love or a protective, obsessive one akin to idolatry. One clue appears at chapter's end. When the Fox delightedly exclaims that Psyche is prettier than any classic beauty, even Aphrodite, Orual is dismayed. Remember that Aphrodite is Ungit. Ever fearful, Orual is certain that Ungit has

---

[5] Lewis, *Surprised by Joy: The Shape of My Early Life* (New York: Harcourt, 1956). 72.

heard. It is ironic that the Fox who speaks against the gods compares Psyche to two Greek gods, for his utterance is a praise, and Orual cannot see that her thoughts are worshipful too.

Two details Lewis includes about Psyche bear greater weight within the plot soon. First, Psyche had a strange, "unchanciest love for all manner of brutes" when she holds a toad. Of all creatures at this point, why would Lewis employ the predictable toad, one that could become a prince? Secondly, in her childish imagination, Psyche predicts she will be a "great, great queen, married to the greatest king of all, and he will build me a castle of gold and amber" on the Grey Mountain, a place she is "half in love with" (23). What does Lewis imply by referencing this fantasy?

Chapter 3
SIGNS OF FOREBODING

"gods do not tell"

REDIVAL'S DALLIANCE AND debacle with the young officer Tarin ends the perpetual pleasant season. Tarin is castrated and sold off as a slave, and Redival is given no choice. The fact that she must now by the King's command always stay with Orual, Psyche, and the Fox is stifling for all. And once again, in the midst of his threats to everyone, the King attacks Orual by saying, "And you goblin daughter, do what you're good for, you'd best...if you with that face can't frighten the men away, it's a wonder" (26). How horrid. At least the King is consistent in his abuse. At the same time, Lewis continues to deepen our sympathy for Orual and to provoke our own thoughts about faces.

Redival's sneering and jeering continue as Glome declines—poor harvest, no marriage for the King, and not an ally in sight. Ever a tattle-tale, Redival is witness to a pregnant mother who approaches young Psyche and asks for a kiss, a boon, especially "Because she said her baby would be beautiful if I [Psyche] did" (27). As the account unfolds, Psyche reveals that it has happened before, and oh, how quickly superstition returns. Orual fears that the gods will be jealous once Redival illustrates how people bow and cast dust on themselves before Psyche. The Fox calmly states that "the divine nature is without jealousy," for "those gods—the sorts of gods you (Orual) are always thinking about—are all folly and lies of poets" (28). Preying on Orual's paranoia, Redival offers to seek the Priest of Ungit's advice. Orual agrees to send her with a necklace from their mother while Redival commands the Fox to find her a young king for a husband. Redival may have been patronizing the Fox, but here she reveals to us all that he is "the real King of Glome" (29). Yes, Redival is a true manipulative brat, but she is essential as she reports the truth as a witness.

Not surprisingly Glome continues to disintegrate. A short rebellion is incited by our young eunuch Tarin's father along with a group of other lords. The King himself rides out to rout them, and Orual describes unnecessary slaughter as the King and his men do not leave off when they should. This furthers the "disaffection" among the people, and Orual claims that the King is now weaker in their eyes. But that's not all. A second poor harvest is apparent as a ravaging plague appears. The Fox is deathly ill, but Orual must take his place working for the King. Though she gains the King's respect, almost like a man, Orual also learns of Glome's dire state. Here, as what appears to be a minor tangent, Lewis reveals that the King and his daughters can only marry divine blood from other royal houses, and the nobles are grumbling that the King is without successor. This plot element is lacking in the original myth. How humans can be divine is not explained but instead assumed. Since only the royal families share divinity, could this be a spiritual part of how we as mankind have Christ within us?

Psyche protectively nurses the Fox back to health, and now Orual reminds us of her claim in the first chapter—that the god is against her. She speaks of the "subtlety" of this god as rumors spread of Psyche's ability, "the beautiful princess could cure the fever by her touch" (30). We recognize the power of rumor, and yet it is almost mixed with a hint of faith, for the people believe Psyche can cure. Sure enough, mobs of sick, smelly people appear outside the palace gates. Orual is once again quick to associate smell with Ungit by inference. As the people demand healing and bread, the King determines that Istra must be sent out to appease the people since so many palace guards are ill. She is dressed as a queen, chapleted and regal, and emerges from the dark palace into the light of day. The people respond as if she's a goddess by kneeling in submission and crying out she's Ungit in the flesh (32).

For the length of the hot day, Psyche touches the people, and they touch her until Psyche grows pale and she herself is carried away to a sick bed. Throughout, the King consistently thinks of himself. When Orual is concerned that these actions will kill Psyche, he reacts with "They'll kill us all if she stops" (32).

As Psyche is feverish, she imagines a gold and amber castle on the edge of the Grey Mountain. She speaks of it frequently and soon grows well. I wonder if it is one of the reasons she recovers. She believes in something greater. Psyche is more beautiful now than ever and has lost a measure of childishness as she gained "a new and severer radiance" (33).

Meanwhile, people in Glome both recover and die, yet we don't know whether those Psyche touched are among the living. Ever distrustful and suspicious, Orual carefully mentions that the gods won't ever tell us. That's the way they are. They are not being mysterious but rather intentional by withholding the truth of what happens. The people continue to leave gifts outside of the palace gates for Psyche, even pigeons which are sacred to Ungit. Orual is worried about Ungit's response, but the Fox assures her that since the Priest is sick, her worries are unfounded. Orual is fearful of Ungit the goddess while the Fox assumes the man the Priest is to be avoided. Interestingly enough, Redival now insists on going to Ungit's temple regularly to make offerings. The Fox and Orual always send a reliable slave with her but simply assume Redival has become pious to acquire a husband and to avoid them for part of every day. When Orual warns Redival not to speak with anyone, Redival tersely responds not to worry—men are just as likely to look at ugly Orual as to look at her since they've all seen Istra now. We clearly hear the sass and jealousy in Redival's bratty voice.

Chapter 4
FICKLE LAND, FICKLE PEOPLE

*"the mob had now learned that a
palace door can be opened by banging on it"*

ORUAL WORRIES ABOUT how the people of Glome will continue to react, fretting about how Ungit might be jealous and about how the Priest and other men could retaliate because of the unprompted worship of Psyche. Sure enough, the desperate people return to the palace gates, demanding food. The King surprisingly gives in and gives out a portion. When he swears that he cannot do that again because the fields won't bear, several voices in the crowd cry out that it's because the King hasn't had a son, "Barren king makes barren land" (36). Immediately, the King signals to an archer to shoot the man who spoke. The man is killed, and the mob flees. But famine has its grip on Glome even in the palace.

Orual is next leaving work with her father in the Pillar Room when she encounters Redival and Batta entering the palace. We haven't seen Batta in several chapters, but true to our first impressions of her, she's as critical and deceitful as ever. Redival first saucily exclaims, "You needn't come looking for me sister-jailer...when did you last see the little goddess?" (36). Oh how we hear the dripping sarcasm! Redival and Batta describe how they saw Psyche on her own going through a back lane of the market place. Batta mimics Psyche picking up her robes as she steps into a house. Orual tries to placate Redival and Batta by assuring them that Psyche is just fine since the people were worshipping her a few days before, but Batta seems insistent on talking, or maybe it's rumor-mongering. Batta must feel it's her duty to report that the plague is worse and that the people just might be saying Psyche spread the illness with her touch. Maybe Batta wants to feel important. Maybe she's the rumour source.

Orual quickly leaves them and goes to the palace porch, awaiting Psyche's return. At the end of the day, Psyche approaches the palace, seeing Orual, and leads her to Orual's own room. Once there, in a moment of natural submission, Psyche lays her head on Orual's knees and sighs that something must be wrong with her because the people are calling her "the Accursed." Like her father, Orual reacts immediately with, "Who would dare? We'll have his tongue torn out?" Psyche relates that she had gone into the city alone to visit her old wet-nurse who was sick with the fever, hoping to bring her healing. All was well until she left that house. Psyche describes how she noticed women pulling their skirts away from her as she passed, how a young boy stared and spat at her, and then most cruelly, how a group of men jeered at her and threw stones, calling her "the Accursed." Psyche had fled but was bewildered by their behavior. She is too young, too innocent to know the fickle and changing nature of the mob.

Here, Orual utters perhaps the most revealing symbolic statement possible: "You healed them, and blessed them, and took their filthy disease upon yourself" (39).

Orual is filled with anger and retaliation, clearly revealing how she sees the people as lower and lesser than herself and the royal household while Psyche had had no qualms about visiting the poor and sick. One moment she helps her people. Six days later she is accused. Reminiscent of Isaiah 53:3-4 and the prophesies of Christ, Psyche has indeed borne the people's sorrows and griefs as they rejected her.

> *He was despised and rejected by men;*
> *a man of sorrows, and acquainted with grief;*
> *and as one from whom men hide their faces*
> *he was despised, and we esteemed him not.*

> *Surely he has borne our griefs*
> *and carried our sorrows;*
> *yet we esteemed him stricken,*
> *smitten by God, and afflicted.* (ESV)

Not only has she become independent of her sister, but Psyche the Accursed has also become a Christian symbol. She is the one who comforts her sister Orual who's furious with the people, and she is the one who discerns a connection between Orual and their father's anger. What's more, Psyche presages negative times to come. Though the sisters enjoy a light meal, they both know some doom is eminent. Orual describes the enduring plague, drought, famine, (even bees were dead!), and scavenging lions preying on dying cattle and sheep. Palace work was more difficult than ever as King Trom continued to fly into rages as neighboring kings pressed him with demands he could not fulfill. He verbally and physically abuses both the Fox and Orual.

As the days pass, the plague lessens, and the palace begins to recover. We hear that the Priest has recovered twice now from the plague, and sure enough, he comes to the palace with his own contingent of guards, almost anticipating a fight. He might be old and blind, but the fear of Ungit still rests upon him as he enters. Two temple girls lead him, and their description is significant. Orual says they are "wooden" with their painted faces and white wigs. Their bare chests or paps, too, are painted gold, and they say nothing. As in Chapter 1, Orual speaks of an "Ungit smell" that invades the room with the mix of incense and smell of old age. It is a "reek" not an aroma. This is the smell she calls "holy." And in one sense, it is. It is an odor that is distinctive, setting apart Ungit and her worship from all others.

Chapter 5
THE PRIEST, THE BRUTE, AND PSYCHE

"Without the shedding of blood there is no forgiveness of sins."
—Hebrew 9:22

THE SCARECROW OF a Priest begins to speak as soon as the King finishes with his overdone welcome. He announces to the King that he and the elders and nobles convened all night in Ungit's temple to discuss what to say to the King about his failing kingdom and his lack of an heir. The King is understandably and predictably outraged yet fearful of the Priest, whom Orual terms "a vulture" (45). In spite of regular sacrifices to Ungit, the Priest insists that the land is impure and thus Ungit requires further expiation for any person identified as "the Accursed." As the Priest elaborates upon three separate instances where citizens spoke against or acted against Ungit and Glome, the Priest's intent is clear—Glome must be rid of the Accursed and sacrificed to the Brute. The King thinks the Brute is but a story of his grandmother's, but the Priest insists that it has been seen again, specifically on the first night the lions returned. Then, the Priest tells the King that Ungit has been speaking to him in the night about "mortals aping the gods" and stealing their worship. Orual immediately recognizes Redival and Batta's influence at the temple. Only their malicious gossip could do such damage, questioning Psyche's actions in the city.

Here, the Fox interrupts by the King's permission and logically questions the appearance of the Brute, declaring that the head shepherd simply saw a shadow behind the lion because of his torch. The Priest responds that that is but Greek wisdom from a slave. Instilling more fear, he insists that the Brute could actually be a shadow and could be hunting in the city even now, though he would not touch the divine blood of the King. The people would fear and come against the King, and so the King must make the Great Offering. The King listens and asks how to make this offering.

In a mysterious way, the Priest describes that the Brute is Ungit OR her son, the god of the mountain. The person chosen as the Great Offering is tied to the Holy Tree on the mountain and left for the Brute. That victim must be perfect, but here the Priest's explanation is cloudy:

> "For, in holy language, a man so offered is said to be Ungit's husband, and a woman is said to be the bride of Ungit's son. And both are called the Brute's supper. And when the Brute is Ungit, it lies with the man, and when it is her son it lies with the woman. And either way there is a devouring...some say the loving and the devouring are all the same thing" (49).

Without a doubt, most of my students respond in disgust to these pagan statements. However, Lewis is clearly describing an act of covenant, a moment of unity where something is both taken and given, a moment where the soul of each bonds together. This may not be a marriage covenant, but it is a sacrifice and sexual union in one act. If we look beyond the pagan shell of this description, then we see how Lewis is shaping a spiritual and Christian parallel. To be one with God, perfect love, requires all we are.

The Priest continues as he declares no ordinary man or woman will do. Now the King is worried that his divine blood will be called to account. The Fox interrupts again, pointing out the illogic of all the Priest has described. In quite an astute manner, the Priest responds carefully that a slave who did not resist when captured was unworthy, let alone because as a Greek he demands to see clearly and is unable to understand holy things, "as if the gods were no more than letters written in a book" (50). Lewis captures a particular sentiment in the Priest's words here—<u>those who think they can logically know the gods and their ways by reading or study, or by some intellectual key, are mistaken. They are limited by their minds</u>. The Priest instead beautifully illustrates how the gods "dazzle our eyes and flow in and out of one another like eddies on a river, and nothing that is said clearly can be said truly about them" (50). If we think we know them, we don't. He continues, "Holy places are dark places. It is life and strength, not knowledge and words, that we get in them. Holy wisdom is not clear and thin like water, but thick and dark like blood" (50). The Priest sounds quite barbaric, yet there is much truth in his words. <u>Dark is not evil, but rather unknown like a limitless place, a place without light by human understanding. Holy wisdom is weighty with many layers and not easily known.</u> In it is life, the life of the blood. Perhaps now as we consider the Priest's words, we can also read the story with God in lieu of Ungit or the gods in general.

The Priest progresses and explains to the King how he and the elders drew lots to determine where the Accursed was within Glome. One by one, he eliminates the common people, the elders, the nobles, and then...the lots fall to the King's house. Trom naturally explodes, ignorantly assuming he's been targeted. What persistent pride! He shouts "Treason!" and calls for Bardia, the captain of the palace guard, venting that all the Priest's guards must be killed. The Priest counters that all of Glome is now in arms surrounding the palace. I can only imagine how the King feels in that moment, when he learns he is the last to know of what happened in the night. The Priest assures Bardia that he would be fighting against Ungit if he obeys the King's orders. In spite of the King's fussing, Bardia says he will not "fight against powers and spirits" (53) as the King calls him a "Girl!"

Bardia is dismissed, and the King turns to the Priest with his knife as Orual and Psyche stand nearby. Holding his dagger to the

Priest's ribs, he threatens to kill the queen wasp. Orual states that the Priest remains miraculously still, without a hint of fear, threatening to haunt the King if he does die. She is sure of the Priest and his faith and expresses that "the room was full of spirits and the horror of holiness" (54). As he confidently proclaims he remains Ungit's voice, the Priest tells them the lots said "no" when asked if the Accursed was the king. True to his character once again, Trom practically smiles with relief, and Orual is disgusted by his selfish reaction, hoping all along that he could see that Psyche would be targeted. The Priest then identifies the Accursed as Psyche. The King feigns sadness, but Orual goes mad. She weeps and begs and clings to the King's feet while he reacts in anger, kicking at her and shouting more insults, unbelievably likening her to cowards and gods and priests and lions, all at once. She lies still at this point, hearing the men plan for Psyche's sacrifice and her imprisonment that night. They coldly spoke of increasing the number of guards against the fickle "weathercocks" of a people, planning for the sacrifice as if it were some typical event. Overwhelmed by emotion, grief, and physical pain, Orual faints.

Chapter 6

THE REALITY OF THE BRAVE AND THE BEAUTIFUL

"if the one weren't so brave and the other so beautiful"

ORUAL COMES TO as the Fox and King help her to a seat. Almost apologizing, her father gives her a bit of wine and some advice for taking care of her bruises, admonishing her that women simply cannot get in the way. Orual reflects that he is indeed "a vile and pitiable king" with the smallest amount of shame for beating her and not defending Psyche (57). When the King then reveals that Psyche will be sacrificed the very next day, Orual is beside herself. The Fox tries to comfort her, saying that this is best, when the King counters and asks the Fox what he would do in all his clever logic. The Fox explains how he would bargain for time, "if he were king and father" (59). Naturally, since Trom is not a true father in the sense of love and care, he argues that the Fox's actions would be extreme— "...your counsel is that I should throw my crown over the roof, sell my country to Phars, and get my throat cut..." (60). With the greatest sarcasm and disdain, the Fox states, "I had forgotten that your own safety was the thing we must work for at all costs" (60). Miraculously, the King either misses or ignores the Fox's impudence. Orual interjects by appealing to the King's pride, telling him that the people might say he was hiding behind a woman, his own daughter. At this, the King reacts in typical Trom anger, exclaiming that it's no wonder he beat Orual, especially since there was no way he could mar her face. Ever verbally abusive, he rages that Psyche is his, and so he has the right to do with her what he wants. He is suspicious of Orual and cannot believe that she loves her half-sister. Trom has now shown us all there is to his person and personality—temper, cruelty, pride, ignorance, selfishness, and a clear inability to understand the nature of love.

As he explains that one must die for many, just as in battle, Orual offers herself to the Brute in Psyche's place. The King then leads her to his floor-length mirror in the Pillar Room and states that Ungit has demanded the best in the land, "and you'd give her that" (62). We know Orual is ugly since she told us in the first chapter, but now the King's behavior is ugly, and it's no wonder that Orual notices her physical pain in the very next sentence.

Servants, temple guards, even Redival, are gossiping and relating the news of the sacrifice. Orual marks this, but even more so, she tells of the presence of Ungit as she smells incense and animal sacrifice outside with "the reek of holiness everywhere" (62). The smell remains synonymous with darkness. Redival rushes forward and gushes about poor Psyche and amazingly says "I didn't mean any harm—it wasn't I," confirming what we already knew from Orual's suspicions. At this, Orual threatens to hang Redival by her thumbs to torture her by a slow fire. Redival is dismayed at Orual's lack of empathy, but Orual knows her shallow sister and knows she is only somewhat chastened, soon to be distracted again by a new bauble or lover.

Now after the King's and Redival's ugly words, Orual again becomes aware of the pain in her side and now her foot, but she hurries as best she can to the room where Psyche is being held. Bardia, captain of the guard himself, is guarding it and will not let Orual enter. He is firm and kind in his refusal to Orual's emotional entreaties. Orual runs away to the King's bedchamber and grabs one of her father's swords, returning to attack Bardia. Without any sign of exertion, Bardia quickly disarms the weak and injured Orual who then collapses, weeping. Bardia at first responds in perhaps a typical virile way by complementing Orual's swordsmanship and bravery rather than acknowledging her tears. Yet as they talk, and Orual even wishes for death, Bardia tenderly comforts her and explains how he rather than a common sentry chose his post. Relenting in spite of the King's commands and

Ungit's demands, Bardia allows Orual inside, thoughtfully saying, "I wonder do the gods know what it feels like to be a man" (66). What an ironic statement at a moment when we know that the pagan gods are just like men in their fickleness and behavior. Instead, we realize that Bardia's statement is more about his caring and merciful nature.

Chapter 7
LAST MOMENTS

"As a young man marries a young woman, so will your Builder marry you; as a bridegroom rejoices over his bride, so will your God rejoice over you." —Isaiah 62:5

ORUAL RUSHES IN to embrace Psyche, yet it is Psyche who comforts Orual, which brings its own measure of pain to Orual's heart. Isn't she, the elder, the Maia or mother, supposed to comfort her sister who's about to be sacrificed? Maia in Greek can mean mother or nurse, but in Greek mythology, Maia is also the oldest and loveliest of the Pleiades, the seven sisters eventually transformed into stars by Zeus.[6] Once again, Lewis deepens a paradoxical moment where the most beautiful Psyche or soul calls her most ugly sister both mother and the loveliest of sisters. Psyche truly sees who her sister is. This is the strongest metaphor for the chapter because Psyche is operating in a reality where she is fully aware of the natural and spiritual planes whereas Orual is limited to her own selfish mindset.

Orual also tells us that as she first sees Psyche, the imprint of the scene is most vivid in her mind—Psyche, a bed, and a lamp. It is a scene that will repeat itself. Psyche is naturally dismayed to see Orual's bruises and injuries as Orual quickly recounts what has happened and calls her father a coward who would hide behind a woman in battle just as he is now as the kingdom is at

---

[6] William Smith, ed. *A Dictionary of Greek and Roman Biography and Mythology.* 1844 (Ann Arbor: U of Michigan, 2005). http://name.umdl.umich.edu/acl3129.0001.001.

such a crux. As they talk, Orual admits to us, the readers, that she is dissatisfied with Psyche's reactions. She is disturbed by Psyche's smile, by the fact that she isn't weeping, by her mimicry of the Fox's mantra, by the fact perhaps that she is not as disturbed by her pending death as Orual is. Psyche encourages Orual to not be rash or think of suicide since they, Orual, the Fox, and Psyche, have been "friends." That word unhinges Orual further as she cries out, "Oh, your heart is of iron" (69). Again, Psyche bolsters Orual, admonishing her and the Fox to stand like two soldiers in battle, to say goodbye to their father for her though it is but a duty, even to remember Redival by giving her all of her gaudy, costly jewels. Orual reacts strongly against this, but Psyche as the voice of wisdom reminds her that she, Orual, wouldn't want to be Redival.

As Orual weeps, Psyche comforts her with the most disturbing words, "You'll break my heart, and I to be a bride" (70). She reminds Orual of the divine blood that flows through them as royalty, a heritage to be proud of. <u>In the same way, the words of the apostle Peter call us a royal priesthood, God's special possession (I Peter 2:9), who are called to be the bride of Christ in John 3. Psyche is not grieving her death as Orual expected but instead sees the beauty of her sacrifice, almost as a bride-price.</u> The only moment Psyche weeps is when she expresses how she doubts her faith, the what-if question of whether the Shadowbrute and the sacrifice are real, whether her death would be senseless.

As she finishes crying, Psyche explains how the Priest of Ungit came to her and made more things clear. She realizes that the Fox only had a limited view of the world, and Orual concurs. It's as if the Fox understood a city on top of the ground but not the depths beneath it (71). Orual, however, takes a negative stance, asserting that the Fox was too good to believe that the gods were real since they are "viler than the vilest men" (71). Psyche counters that the gods just might be real and that they might not be doing the things we accuse them of as if we don't understand them. Orual confesses to the readers that this type of talk angers her even more. She selfishly wants Psyche to talk of their love, their grief, over parting because it "seemed to cost her so little" (71). Orual cannot stop herself from being the most negative, yelling that the people want the Brute to murder her. Psyche calmly responds that she knows she will die, even calling herself a ransom for Glome. How else can she go to the gods or be with a god unless she dies in her humanness? <u>Psyche sees herself as a ransom while Orual sees her as a scapegoat</u>. Orual again violently and selfishly reacts, asking Psyche how their relationship could mean so little. Orual cannot see what Psyche is describing, yet Psyche is the most realistic. She explains to Orual how their best time on earth has come and gone. What real future do they have as the daughters of the King of Glome?

In utter honesty, Psyche further reveals how she has always longed for death. By this, she means that in the purest and happiest moments of childhood when she, Orual, and the Fox were on the hills far from the palace and city and nearest the Grey Mountain, she felt an invitation to go. It was such a strong yearning yet she couldn't identify what it was until now. Orual bitterly realizes that the sacrifice has already begun.

Orual interrupts her narrative and reminds us of why she is writing this book, as an accusation against the gods and also as a confessional against herself. And so, she confesses that she was full of a grudging sin. Orual didn't want Psyche to comfort herself with these words and explanations. Instead she is full of a grieving anger.

In the midst of this, Psyche recalls with wonder a beautiful imagination of a gold and amber palace built by a wonderful king. She sees herself as perfectly chosen and prepared because any other in Glome would be filled with terror and misery at the prospect. <u>Much like Song of Solomon 2, Psyche is filled with anticipation at meeting her beloved as he calls to her.</u> Full of faith, she has always longed for this home and knows she was meant for this. Stupidly, Orual only sees that Psyche doesn't remember her or their sweet times as but a small part of her life. Orual chooses to take offense and lashes out that Psyche never loved her. Bardia interrupts with a knock at the door, and Orual must leave with a last "spoiled embrace," one she singlehandedly spoiled.

Chapter 8
POMP AND CIRCUMSTANCE

*"To love, and lose what we love,
are equally things appointed for our nature."*

AS ORUAL LEAVES the prison room, she notes the pains from the beating by her father, yet Orual is determined to join the sacrifice procession. Once she learns it is to begin before dawn, she retires to her room feeling "a great dullness and heaviness" (77). Though she could eat but little, Orual is put to bed by her maidservants only to wake a few hours later in excruciating pain as her eye has swollen shut and her bruised or broken bones have stiffened. Weeping, her women help her to dress.

Soon, music is heard, and Orual descends with much help to the Great Hall. The scene before her is most dramatic. Scores of guards, nobles, and temple girls gather within while the mob is without. Orual eerily describes the noble girls who are veiled and wreathed like a bridal party, her father in his best robes, the Priest in his full bird mask, the lingering smell of sacrifice, but worst of all is her glimpse of Psyche. She resembles a temple girl painted gold and wearing a wig, stiff and practically lifeless. Immediately, Orual blames the gods, saying that they are killing Psyche after having stolen her—

> "It was not enough for the gods to kill her; they must make her father the murderer. It was not enough to take her from me, they must take her three times over, tear out my heart three times. First her sentence; then her strange, cold talk last night; and now this painted and gilded horror to poison my

last sight of her. Ungit had taken the most beautiful thing that was ever born and made it into an ugly doll" (80).

Orual never makes it down the stairs to the great hall. She falls and is carried back to her rooms as the procession leaves. For days after, she is sick and delusional. Orual blames the gods in her dreams, for she feels they force her to claim that Psyche is now her enemy instead of her greatest love.

Eventually Orual recovers and remembers Psyche had done her no wrong, yet Orual does begrudge her for spending so much time speaking about everyone else but herself in their last moments. This jealousy, this selfishness, does not fade. Orual doesn't dwell on what had happened to Psyche. She thinks only of herself. Outside of her small focus, the rains had returned to Glome the day after the sacrifice, and Orual learns that the Fox and her women have ever been by her side throughout her sickness—"I was loved; more than I thought" (83). Love is a rare word for Orual, so even this mention reveals more of her sensitivity as she is physically and emotionally weakened. Glome too is on the mend as the grasses and cattle revive, birds return, and the last of the sickness fades. But as the Fox relays what Orual has missed, a sourness lingers. He speaks of how her father had become "the darling" of the people since he had put on a good show at Psyche's sacrifice. Orual is not at all surprised and calls him a mountebank, much like a snake-oil salesman. The Fox defends him, saying that Trom's tears could have been as real as anyone's. In other news, the neighboring kingdom of Phars is in a minor civil war over their king's successor, so Glome has nothing to fear politically, but there, the chit-chat stops.

Days later, Orual bluntly asks the Fox if he still feels that Ungit and her legends are but lies of priests and poets. He thinks so, but Orual counters that everything changed after Psyche's sacrifice. Is that not proof that Ungit is real? In an emotional scene, the Fox mutters that it is cursed chance or coincidence that reinforces barbarian beliefs like this, yet he next explains how chance cannot exist because we are all part of one web. One simple thread, such as an ocean wind, came from miles away at the right time to bring rain to Glome. Orual is not comforted. What if the King had waited a few days more? The Fox insists that the King's and people's deeds were ignorant and evil, but Psyche wasn't. The Fox wasn't there, but he was told that Psyche remained calm without weeping, even when everyone left. As he describes the scene to Orual, he breaks down in grief and has to leave her— "his love got the better of his philosophy," states Orual (85). How true and real.

The Fox is all logic and level-headed the next day. He reasons that loving and losing love are all part of human nature. Didn't Psyche die with everything she could ever want, even a moment of fame like the Greek heroines Iphigenia or Antigone? In the tales of the Trojan War, Iphigenia was sacrificed to the gods by her father King Agamemnon in exchange for his fleet's safe passage as they headed to Troy. Full of faith, Antigone was known for obeying the gods' laws above men's as she determined to bury her forsaken brother. These famed women had no doubts that the gods were real and active, yet ironically Orual invites the Fox to tell the full tales once again as he finds comfort in the telling. The next morning Orual announces that she can be Antigone too, and so she determines to ascend the Grey Mountain to bury what remains of Psyche. How ironic that she identifies with Antigone most as if she can obey the gods' laws, the very gods that she has accused from the beginning for obscuring the fact that they are real. Orual might be fulfilling a duty, but she absolutely does not have the faith of Antigone, or for that matter, Psyche.

Chapter 9
DIFFERENT TRUTHS

"everything was changed"

ORUAL BEGINS TO plan a return to Psyche's place of sacrifice on the mountain. Still regaining her strength, she has eluded her father's demands and has not returned to work in the Pillar room. He has apparently made even more of his love for Psyche and is aggravated by the survival of his "hobgoblin" and "whore" daughters. Orual so desires to see the site and bury Psyche's bones, yet she knows her life is purposeless after this task is done. Hers is a reality of dread and hope, a purgatory Orual describes as "deadness" (89).

One afternoon Orual listlessly walks about the palace grounds when Bardia interrupts her reverie. Acknowledging her grief and hoping to help her, Bardia advises her to train with him in swordfighting. After all, in their quick spat outside of Psyche's room, he saw skill and promise. Orual reluctantly consents and soon passes a half hour of distracting work with "sweat as the kindest creature...far better than philosophy, as a cure for ill thoughts" (91). After the exercises, Orual accidentally hears an exchange between Bardia and another soldier when Bardia replied, "Why yes, it's a pity about her face. But she's a brave girl and honest. If a man was blind and she weren't the King's daughter, she'd make him a good wife" (92). Oh, how kind and cruel, and Orual ironically terms it "the nearest thing to a love-speech that was ever made me" (92). We know Bardia intended no harm, still once again Orual's ugliness is bluntly acknowledged. Just as any author repeats a description or concept for emphasis, Lewis drives this truth as a mallet hits a spike repeatedly. Anyone can see Orual's ugliness on the outside. Maybe now we begin to wonder about ourselves. Could Lewis be asking us to examine our own ugliness?

Since Orual finds relief and healing in this physical training, she continues to work with Bardia. One day, she speaks of her need to go to the mountain. Bardia understands and insists on going with her because he can ride and protect her. They plan for one night on the mountain, and Orual teases him that the King won't let him go. In an unusual moment, Bardia explains that he can spin a yarn and that the King is easy to get along with. Orual is perplexed because she had not seen this aspect of her father.

Six days later, Bardia and Orual leave on his horse in the pre-dawn hours. Orual is wearing a full hooded cloak complete with a veil to hide her face. This is the second time in the story that she wears a veil. We know she doesn't want to be recognized on this secret journey. She also wears her short sword since Bardia cautions her about the wild creatures they could encounter, and she carries an empty urn for Psyche's remains. They make their way silently through the sleeping city, cross the Shennit river, and head for the mountain road as the clouds break and the sun rises. Filled with momentary dread, Orual describes Ungit's temple as they pass by: like a fat slug, it lies crudely constructed of large stones with a domed thatched roof, resembling an oval egg with constant smoke rising from the flame to Ungit. The priests call it a holy shape and say it is "the egg from which the whole world was hatched or the womb in which the whole world once lay" (94). But this story, like other ancient ones about the creation of the world, may not be meant to be understood. It simply could be man's attempt to explain what he does not know. Orual does not even try to interpret this statement but is filled with relief and a lightening as they pass into the foothills and wilderness. Bardia chooses to go off of the path where the procession would have led Psyche, and they ascend the steepening slopes.

As they top a ridge and can actually see the mountain in front of them, Orual says "everything changed. And my struggle began"

(95). Orual surveys a most colorful landscape of little lakes, valleys, hills, woods, and cliffs that bring delight to her. Yet, she is torn by the grief of her errand and the beauty and hope of the scene before her. "Why does your heart not dance?" she thinks. Can she allow herself this lightening of grief? Can the world outside of the palace truly be so beautiful and full of wonder? Can she see the difference between the choice of selfishness or the choice of joy exactly as it was presented to her in her last moments with Psyche?

The paradox returns, and it is her second invitation to choose. "Who can feel ugly when the heart meets delight?" (96). Weighing her logic, self-control, and these momentary delights, Orual wrestles with these thoughts as they continue. She affirms that this is a "god-haunted, plague-breeding, decaying, tyrannous world" and she knows not to trust the beauty and light she momentarily enjoys. Assuming the worst, Orual states, "The gods never send us this invitation to delight so readily or so strongly as when they are preparing some new agony. We are their bubbles; they blow us big before they prick us" (97). She clearly steels herself with a measure of self-control as she and Bardia near the final ascent.

Past the tree line now, they see a black valley of stone and scree, "as if the Mountain had sores," they must cross as they face a mouth of rock wall. Dismounting, they head to a lower "saddle" where they can see the lone, leafless tree. Ever filled with dread of the unknown, Orual and Bardia approach. They find the iron belt used to chain Psyche to the tree but no human trace. Bardia insists only the god, the Shadowbrute, has taken her. Only he could remove her with her clothing and jewels without a trace. Orual feels an emptiness. If there is nothing to bury or remove, what is there to do? She suggests they search for any remnant about the tree, and Bardia soon finds a ruby he knew to be part of Psyche's sandals. Orual is encouraged and wants the search to continue, but Bardia explains that he best do it because to go farther beyond the saddle or rock ridge is to go into the gods' country. Not even priests go so far.

Orual insists she join him, so they collect the horse and carefully ascend the ridge. As they crest it, the formerly hidden sun emerges in brightness and reveals below them an astounding jewel of a valley—bush and vine bloom, trees flourish, water pools and cascades, the air warm. Bardia reverently calls the haven "the secret valley of the god" (101). They descend into this Eden. As Orual stops to drink at the first creek and pushes aside her veil, she hears Bardia and another voice cry out. She quickly looks up, and in shock, sees Psyche herself across the water.

Orual's movements are no accident. It is in this exact moment AS the sun shines so brightly, AS she lowers herself in humility to drink of the god's water, AS she temporarily moves the veil that Orual both hears and then sees her sister in reality. <u>The veil that stands between her and life, this growing symbol of facade, is noticeably gone.</u>

Chapter 10
JOY AND FAITH

"Have you no wonder?"

CRYING AND LAUGHING, Orual is wild with joy at seeing Psyche. Bardia, however, is frightened beyond belief, assured it is her ghost. Psyche appears different as she is tan and lean and wearing the rags of her dress now. Orual calls her "brightface," for she is laughing, full of joy herself, as she welcomes her Maia. As Psyche invites Orual to cross the stream, she commands Bardia to remain, which he does gladly. Though he's unsure if Orual should go, she's insistent, and he responds with something we've heard before: "Of course. It's not with you as with us. You have gods' blood in you. I'll stay here . . ." Previously, the idea of divine blood was mentioned because the princesses could only marry royalty said to descend from the gods, a completely Greek thought. Now though, Bardia's fear-filled reaction shows us a deeper meaning. As one of the people, Bardia expresses the truth he knows—the divine blood is real, and he is full of fear and awe and a measure of faith.

Orual fords the mountain stream with Psyche's help, and the sisters joyfully reunite, soon sitting down to partake of a mountain banquet. Psyche describes a handful of mountain berries and water as delicacies fit for the gods while Orual thinks Psyche is playing a delightful childhood game. Immediately Orual asks what they should do but Psyche counters with "...be merry! Why should our hearts not dance?" It's as if Orual were Martha busily planning and doing just as Psyche is Mary, full of eagerness, rest, and delight. Psyche even says, "Solemn Orual, you were always one for plans" (105).

Again, Psyche comforts Orual who begins thinking of all that could have happened to Psyche, and Psyche relates all that has truly happened since the day of sacrifice. Almost like an audience, we see her getting dressed, painted, and drugged like one of the temple girls. It was all like a dream, and interestingly enough, Psyche not only describes seeing Orual at the top of the stairs but also tells her she, Orual, was in a dream practically. What's more, Psyche states that Orual is now almost awake! What could that mean? Orual doesn't interrupt, and Psyche offers no interpretation as her story resumes.

In this drug-induced state, Psyche recounts how the journey was both brief and yet interminable. As the drugs wear off, she tries to speak in a mumble, and she is drugged again as the procession reaches the tree. Psyche is fastened to the tree with an iron belt and chain as the King weeps and wails. We would assume this is just another show for him, but Psyche insists that he was truly seeing her for the first time. Does it take imminent death for the King to realize who she is as his daughter?

Finally, the King, priest, and people leave, and Psyche is alone. She describes crying for a time before a number of creatures visit her. First, the lean mountain cattle come and go, then a lynx, yet nothing else. Though she tries to comfort herself with her imagination of the god and his amber palace, Psyche realizes that those longings are absolutely gone. Orual inwardly rejoices and thinks later that this could be one other reason the gods are against her. As Psyche continues, Orual seems to always question the reality of what Psyche is saying. <u>Doubt is a reflex for her.</u>

Then, the weather shifts, and the wind and rains come. Psyche declares that "the gods really are, and that I was bringing the rain" (110). Soon, as the wild wind increases, Psyche exclaims that she saw the West Wind, the god himself. She felt insignificant beside him, and he pulled her out of the iron belt and left her in the secret valley. Orual is incredulous as Psyche vows and insists her experience was real. Still fearful to a degree and in awe of the god's presence, she hears voices welcome her to HER house as they call her "the bride of the god." Like the original myth, these voices or spirits bathe, feed, and entertain her in the palace. Psyche feels insufficient next to them and explains that she would be like a dream in contrast to the waking world. That is how a mortal feels next to an immortal. After the evening banquet, her husband would come in the night to her.

Orual is jarred out of her doubt and exclaims, "If this is true, then I've been wrong all my life!" (115). Thus, if the gods are real according to Psyche, her soul, then Orual must see them and this palace. She sounds much like Thomas demanding to see Jesus, "Unless I see in his hands the mark of the nails, and place my finger into the mark of the nails, and place my hand into his side, I will never believe" (John 20:25). As Orual demands to see the palace. Psyche is horribly crushed because they have been standing on the palace steps the entire time.

Chapter 11
THE INVITATION

"For you, it is not there at all"

ORUAL HERSELF TELLS us this is a most critical moment because her charge against the gods hinges on this stalemate. Shocked for different reasons, Psyche and Orual are completely silent. Orual thinks of shutting the door in her mind to prevent something from coming in. Could this mean she might possibly believe Psyche or at least want to believe her? Though Orual insists they leave the valley, Psyche assumes she can see the palace and that's why she wants to leave. They argue. Psyche wants Orual to feel an actual palace wall, and Orual reacts in anger by shaking her by the shoulders. Psyche demands an explanation. Why did Orual praise the wine and honeycakes she gave if they weren't real? Orual tells us she had only drunk water from Psyche's hands and eaten berries, and yet I can't help but think of the door in her mind she needed to shut. Is it possible that Orual did taste of the fruits of the palace and knew it? If so, she's determined not to tell Psyche or us the truth.

With sudden understanding, Psyche recalls the words of her husband and realizes Orual can not see. And with this statement, Orual declares she "almost came to a full belief" (120). She knows Psyche is certain, and she knows she, Orual, is not. It is a sickening feeling, and Orual is filled with both horror and grief at the gulf between them, immediately blaming the gods. Their job must be to cause pain and separation. Orual cries out, "It's not right. Oh, Psyche, come back!" She does, and they sit for a few moments as once again Psyche comforts her sister. She explains that she will beg her husband to help Orual see. But as Psyche mentions him—

"my god, my lover, my husband"—Orual is enraged and determines that Psyche must be insane, especially because she has not seen him. Even more so, Orual witnesses the "unspeakable joy" in Psyche's eyes as she speaks of her husband. Orual still wants to take her away, but Psyche employs logic and asks her to consider how she looks, telling Orual that she will again ask her husband for help. Orual reacts and yells, "I don't want it!" As observers, we know that Orual is implicitly acknowledging Psyche's reality even if it is painful. She cries out that she hates this darkness, this type of confusion. <u>Maybe it's the pain of stepping from unbelief into faith, but Orual cannot and will not do it.</u>

Orual badgers Psyche, demanding she leave, insulting her as she compares her to a temple girl. Psyche is not swayed and declares, "You must come to me" (125). Issued as both a command and invitation, this is Orual's point of choice. Yes, Orual thinks it is madness, and faith indeed must appear so in the natural. But then, it begins to rain. Orual offers her cloak as protection for she sees Psyche getting wet. But Psyche patiently discloses that they are inside. Orual then "saw in a flash that I must choose one opinion or the other; and in the same flash knew which I had chosen" (126). She has chosen not to believe and still again tries to reason with Psyche, first offering the approaching winter as an excuse and then trying to command her as a child. Psyche reiterates that she is a wife who obeys her husband, and Orual grabs her arm, trying to pull her away. But Psyche is stronger. Physical force cannot sway her. Psyche promises to work on her behalf and tells Orual to leave now that the sun is setting. She gently leads Orual to the river and helps her cross. Orual cannot stop begging, offering to become beggar women together wandering in the world or hiding Psyche in Bardia's house. Ever patient, Psyche maintains she is a wife and is happy and leaves Orual there in the deep twilight.

Chapter 12
TWILIGHT

"I saw"

TWILIGHT REPRESENTS SO much in myth—a moment between light and dark, a moment between realities, but especially a moment between what is real and what is supernatural. I've often thought Lewis considered the twilight of the gods as described in Norse mythology, a cataclysmic moment when the world and many of the gods die before a flood. By employing a time of day latent with otherworldliness, could he be foreshadowing the end of the pagan gods, the plural status existing in the barbarian world of Glome?

In the gray light as the sun set, Orual reunites with Bardia who has been waiting for her. He had prepared a campfire and meal before they lie down for the night. Orual reveals that even as they lay back to back for warmth, Bardia would not have thought of her as a woman because "if you are ugly enough, all men (unless they hate you deeply) soon give up thinking of you as a woman at all" (131). Orual cannot sleep. She is full of thoughts and worries and the ever-present *riddle*—are the gods real? What happens next is a critical point in her life. She gets up in the morning twilight, pacing, and makes her way to the river for a drink. Since we know Orual is speaking in retrospect, she introduces the idea that the water flowing through the gods' secret valley could have either brought clarity or confusion. After she kneels for a drink, she looks up and in the mist can see the most unique structure of Psyche's palace. Orual begins to imagine Psyche lying in the arms of her husband and immediately determines to go to the palace steps and beg forgiveness from both him and Psyche. What a sudden change in thought! She must believe the god is real then. Yet, in a single moment, Orual confesses next "if what I saw was real" (133). Doubt creeps in, and as she stands, the sight of the palace fades away in the mist and fog.

Orual interrupts her narrative to remind us again of her original complaint against the gods. She asks us, her readers, to pass judgment. Is this in fact a sign from the gods? Why would they use a sign she asks. Isn't a sign just another riddle anyway? Why would the gods think something she saw in the twilight could produce a clearer belief? Is this just a test? More than anything, she longs for clarity and directness.

Here, as believers, we understand Orual's conundrum. Don't we share these same moments in our relationship with God, moments of doubt, moments of fleeting conviction, moments where we long for a direct instruction from God Himself? "Just speak to me," we think in frustration. Another thought is that Lewis' choice of the word *riddle* might parallel Paul's use of the word *mystery* in Ephesians 1. In that passage, Paul is explaining what Christ's sacrifice has brought us. We are chosen by God, adopted, forgiven, and lavished with grace, a grace that "makes known to us the mystery of His will" (Ephesians 1:9 ESV). Most translations use the word *mystery*, but the Complete Jewish Bible overtly employs *secret plan*. God's secret plan is made known to us. Could this be the riddle Orual is seeking to solve?

<u>Orual chooses not to reveal any of this to Bardia. This in itself leads us to think she knows what she saw was real.</u> If she had described what she saw to him, Bardia out of fear would have immediately concurred the palace was real based on his superstitious beliefs and fear of the place. Maybe this is why Orual doesn't. Bardia cannot be objective.

They begin the return journey down to Glome. As they progress, Orual determines to tell Bardia the story of what happened, intentionally excluding the moment and truth of seeing the palace. When she asks him what he thinks of all that happened, Bardia insists he is pious and faithful and would never intentionally offend the gods— "I think the less Bardia meddles with the gods, the less they'll meddle with Bardia" (135). What is Lewis showing us then? <u>What type of believer or follower is Bardia?</u>

Continuing to lie about the palace, Orual persistently peppers Bardia with questions. She manipulates him, appealing to his bravery and his wise insight and finally draws some thoughts out of him. Bardia thinks perhaps the Brute must be ugly or frightful or she wouldn't be forbidden to see him. It's no riddle to him. This just confirms Orual's dark suspicions. She's positive the people would agree. The gods got what they wanted and so relieved Glome of its troubles. Yet, her thoughts grow ever darker: "something, so foul it would not show itself, some holy and sickening thing, ghostly or demonlike or bestial—or all three (there's no telling with gods)—enjoyed her at its will" (137). Orual thinks of the quickest solution. Kill Psyche, and the issue is resolved. This thought brings tears and more variables. Orual wants to fix everything. Should she interfere? Wasn't Psyche happy?

As an observer then, I think to myself, <u>if Psyche might represent the soul or the part of us that does have faith, what is Orual saying? Would we consider "killing" that part of us because we don't understand ourselves or allow understanding of our soul?</u> The questions continue, but Orual has made a decision. I wouldn't call it a choice. Psyche will not be "sport for a demon," and Orual says she would kill her out of love. "I perceived now that there is a love deeper than theirs who seek only the happiness of their beloved" (138). So Orual's view of love twists and perverts even further as she returns to the palace.

Chapter 13
JUSTIFICATION

*"My terrible temptation came back;
to leave her to that fool-happy dream..."*

THE FOX WAS waiting, like most foxes do. Orual announces that Psyche is alive and well, and she will tell him everything once she has eaten and dried herself. Here, we also meet Orual's only named slave, Poobi. In my classes, my students always laugh at her name. After a few years of this reaction, I'm now inclined to think Lewis introduces her, or more aptly, her name as comic relief. What humor to introduce a character who cannot speak to us yet whose name causes a giggle or two.

The sweet and sour comes, as Orual calls it. One minute she tells the Fox that Psyche is alive and happy even, the next she reveals the entire story, minus her glimpse of the palace. The Fox is understandably crushed, assured Psyche is mad. Suddenly, Orual introduces the thought that all is not as it appears: "you don't think...there might be things that are real because we don't see them?" (141). Most of us would assume a discussion of faith is imminent. Instead, we return to the comfortable world of philosophy and logic. The Fox slips into analytical mode and answers Orual first with things we logically can't see, like abstract concepts and things in the dark, even the concept of the human soul. But Orual is not sidetracked. She knows what the Fox means by the soul. She wants to know what else could exist. As they argue further, Orual must know what it is that comes to Psyche in the dark. The Fox logically asserts it must be a man, specifically a mountain man, outlaw, or vagabond living on the mountain. Orual seems genuinely shocked, yet minutes before she had toyed with telling the Fox what she had really seen, meaning she knows that the god, Psyche's husband, is real. Could she really be surprised by his conclusion?

Convinced by the idea of a mountain man, the Fox reasons through the entire scenario. Yes, a man has freed Psyche, told tales, and led her into a fantasy world. Orual is amazed at how plausible this scenario is just as Bardia's version seemed as real. Oh Orual, how easily you are led, how hard you fight to believe what you truly saw.

The Fox is still perplexed about what to do, how to help Psyche, how to solve the riddle. Lewis uses the word *riddle* again, as if there is something to figure out. But is there? Isn't this further irony when compared to Orual's use of the word? Meanwhile, the King will be away hunting lions for several days, and Orual is determined to return to the mountain. The Fox again logically states that Psyche will soon be with child as winter approaches. Reacting in utter anger, Orual furiously refutes the thought. A mere man mingle with the divine blood of their house! Again, the Fox and Orual discuss what to do, whether to hide Psyche or send her away. The Fox is sure she would be sacrificed again if the people of Glome saw her. Orual counters that Psyche wouldn't leave anyway. She was too insistent, and they would need force, but Orual must "overrule" her, convince her of "her shame and danger" (147).

Orual continues to rant, and we wonder how she could so quickly set aside the truth. Is she so easily swayed? The Fox wonders the same. He is amazed at her anger, her passions, and especially her declaration that she would rather kill Psyche than leave her to some man. He calms her as only he can: "Daughter, daughter. You are transported beyond all reason and nature. Do you know what it is? There's one part love in your heart, and five parts anger, and seven parts pride" (148). The Fox is so accurate! What is it in Orual that drives her to fix the riddle of Psyche? Is it not pride first and foremost? Orual continues dramatically, raging about the man forcing or deceiving her, calling him "a runaway slave" or "filth." The Fox takes this personally and responds that he is but the same. Orual calms him, assuring him that he is ten times her father. They next speak of the divine blood of the royal house. Orual is sure the Fox does not believe in it, and in most ways, he does not. <u>He does offer some traditional Stoicism though, stating that the divine is in all men, even the man who has Psyche.</u>

Suddenly, the Fox becomes weary and retires for the night. Orual seems to think he is avoiding the discussion and sees his choice for sleep as a weakness. She's convinced that a woman, or a woman who loves you, would not have done so. The riddle must be solved. Orual's thoughts and accusations continue to deteriorate once the Fox leaves. "Surely everyone has left me! Surely no one truly cares for Psyche!" She is alone and full of a sense of abandonment. She must solve the riddle and will probably guess wrong, so fatalistically sure is she of the vindictive gods.

Once she dismisses Poobi to bed, Orual lays prostrate on the floor and prays to the gods by herself. She repents, she vows, she promises, and hears nothing. Feeling she is left alone, Orual determines to do something in the morning. After a short sleep, she acknowledges that both Bardia and the Fox have strong theories. But these theories only exacerbate her dilemma. She calls it being "the child of Glome and a pupil of the Fox" (151). Only, Orual now sees that she knows it is a possibility that the "man" could in fact be good. However she justifies her actions, Orual feels a need to be stern and forcible with her love. Isn't that what real love is?

Chapter 14
THE CHALLENGE

"Nothing that's beautiful hides its face."

MORNING ARRIVES, THE King has left, and so must Orual. Her packing list is most unique. Again she brings the urn originally intended for Psyche's remains, but now places a lamp, a jar of oil, some linen cloth, and food in it. She eats, then hiding under veil and cloak, departs to find Bardia. Bardia must disappoint her. He cannot be her companion on this second secret mission because he is in charge of the palace while the King is away. He can, however, entrust her to Gram, a small, dark, quiet soldier who is able to ride a horse and accompany her. I wonder at Lewis' dry choice of names again. Does he call Bardia's man a gram because of his size? Just a thought.

Orual asks for a dagger from Bardia, who wonders at her choice, then she leaves to meet Gram. Twice, Lewis hints that Gram fears Orual. Her veil is still on, and we notice that she does not attempt to ameliorate Gram's anxiety. Traveling through rain and wind, Gram and Orual arrive at the secret valley, where light has broken through as it did on the first journey. <u>As an archetype, light often means revelation, that things are made clear. I wonder if that is so for Orual.</u>

Leaving Gram, Orual begins to ford the mountain river and calls out for Psyche who appears immediately. Orual reveals, perhaps in the light of the valley, that they were "two images of love, the happy and the stern—she so young, so brightface, joy in her eye and limbs—I, burdened and resolute, bringing pain in my hand" (157). Yes, Orual can see the contrast and understands it, at least on the surface. She herself says she has no doubt.

Psyche again calls Orual "Maia" or mother, beautiful, reminding her that she would return regardless of the King. I wonder if this could be a return to her own soul (psyche), her own beauty, a true love. Yet Orual shrugs it off and launches into a rehearsed speech about how she is the only one left who loves Psyche and can be trusted to help her, "all the father and mother and kin...and all the King too" (158). Understandably confused, Psyche assures her that her love for Orual is as strong as ever, even stronger since she has learned to love her husband also. She speaks of a deeper, unselfish love. Orual, however, describes a love that hurts, pulling the thorn out. Obviously, Orual views Psyche as a child still who needs nursing, who needs guidance from her childish choices. Psyche responds in strength and maturity that her husband will guide her, not Orual.

Orual thinks that she has the upper hand and pushes Psyche to answer the question as to why the god will not allow his face to be seen. Using "Greek wisdom," Orual follows the traditional rhetorical appeals with logic first. "Think, Psyche," she states, "Nothing that's beautiful hides its face" (160). Orual calls her to think and recognize the facts at the same time stirring her emotions, appealing to pathos. Psyche is still. Why doesn't Orual consider or see her quietness? She reaches for Psyche's hand, and Psyche pushes it away, announcing that she has forgiven her already. Though angry at Orual's accusations about her husband, Psyche has calmed herself and asks Orual to put aside these thoughts because she loves her. Badgering yet, Orual is not swayed and makes an appeal to authority, a certain fallacy, not logic this time. She claims the wisdom and insight of the Fox and Bardia, how both agree Psyche's husband is not who he says he is. Psyche is crushed, "I gave you no leave...it was more like Batta than you" (161). Ah, now Psyche retaliates. Calling Orual a drunken, slovenly gossip should have hurt, but Orual treads on and says all the people of Glome would agree with her, another fallacy normally termed bandwagon. Psyche refutes this, saying that she is his wife, why does it matter to them, why should it matter? By this point, we the readers feel as if we are in a courtroom witnessing the prosecutor attacking a victim. Orual is relentless, using every bit of ammunition, and Psyche must defend herself. If only Orual was in the audience. She would then see our pity and empathy rise to surround Psyche, not her. This stern, tough love is not lovely to watch.

Psyche exclaims that she doesn't have to see her husband: "...how could I not know?" (162). She has been with him intimately. Not a part of her relationship is made up. She knows he is real. Orual doesn't care and demands a test, a challenge—to shine her lamp in the middle of the night and look at the Brute for herself. Psyche insists that the god has expressly forbidden this, yet Orual insults Psyche, calling her a tramp along with Redival, the temple girls, and the King's' lovers. How is this tough love? Orual lets her passions rule her logic as the Fox said. Orual thinks it is fear that holds Psyche back from the test, but Psyche corrects her again. She would be ashamed to disobey because she loves him.

Now the sun is setting. Light fades, and so too any hope of understanding. Orual pleads with Psyche to selfishly free her from her fears, and Psyche remains firm that she cannot. At this, Orual dramatically pulls out her dagger and stabs herself through her arm. What manipulation! Love is something to be forced? Psyche is astounded. Orual calls her to grab the linen in the urn to wrap her wound. We now know that she planned this all along. It wasn't a Plan B but much more. Orual demands a blood oath from Psyche, coercing her. Psyche clarifies that she is more concerned about Orual's life than her own:

> "You are indeed teaching me about kinds of love I did not know. It is like looking into a deep pit. I am not sure whether I like your kind better than hatred. Oh Orual—to take my love for you, because you know it goes down to my very roots and cannot be diminished by any newer love, and then to make

of it a tool, a weapon, a thing of policy and mastery, an instrument of torture—I begin to think I never knew you. Whatever comes after, something that was between us dies here" (165).

Orual does not reflect upon Psyche's words for even the barest of moments. Ignorant Orual demands Psyche's oath or she will kill them both. Is she incapable of understanding Psyche's meaning then? Psyche further explains that spilling blood on her threshold was the most effective threat. This implies that even in ignorance and in the shadows of fading light, Orual had managed to stand on the very entrance to the palace she pretends not to see. The irony continues.

Orual holds out the bloody dagger, and Psyche takes the blood oath. Reminiscent of Hebrews 9:22, Psyche has forgiven Orual through the shedding of blood. But what does Orual's blood accomplish? As in Chapter 2, Orual may only know of blood spilled in anger or sacrifice, just like her father and just like Ungit. And though Orual was granted light in the secret valley, she chose not to see. It is very much a contrast to I John 1:7: *But if we walk in the light, as he is in the light, we have fellowship with one another, and the blood of Jesus, his Son, purifies us from all sin.* But Psyche is able to see this. In addition to the love she will betray, she declares that likely all happiness will be destroyed, all for Orual, "the price you have put upon your life" (166). Orual weeps and leaves the valley as darkness falls.

Chapter 15
AFTERMATH

"You also shall be Psyche."

IT'S TIME TO return to the original myth. In the Greek story, Psyche received her two unnamed sisters at her golden palace on the mountain. Yes, they saw the literal palace. They were awed by its magnificence and the attendants' voices and thus filled with envy, for she had "so much exceeding their own." When they realized that Psyche had never seen her husband, they filled her mind with dark suspicions. Psyche resisted these persuasions for a time, but they did not fail to have their effect, and when her sisters were gone, their words and her own curiosity were too strong for her to resist. Psyche made the choice to disobey her husband in the Greek version. In Lewis's tale, Psyche is stronger. She is not tempted to see her husband, but rather feels forced to comply out of love for her sister. She would rather Orual live than die. Lewis's implications about the nature of love continue.

Orual rests and waits in the dark on the other side of the river, mulling over the possibilities as she waits to witness a light shine in the palace. She begins with the best case scenario. Psyche would shine the light and then would come across the river, whispering for "Maia!" Orual would dramatically rush out to hold and comfort her, and Psyche would once again love her. But darker thoughts come too. If the god was real, then she was sending Psyche to her doom, "robbed of all joy" (169). Orual is tempted to right this wrong, but holds herself back, anxious about Psyche's "un-love" for her. Within moments, Orual sees the first light shine and disappear. She retreats to her imagination again as the bitter cold and the pain of her wound make her realize that she could die. Picturing her own funeral, she revels in the thought of Psyche, Bardia, and the Fox mourning her as they express the depth of their love for her.

But the light shines a second time in utter stillness. A golden, great voice cries out in sternness. Full of fear, Orual recognizes in her mortality that it is immortal. After its speech comes Psyche's weeping, and Orual simply states her "heart broke then" (171). Not only does Orual hear the great voice for herself, but she also sees the great light, a light that reveals a display of power. Lightning strikes repeatedly, felling trees amidst the thunder while the mountains themselves break away in pieces. The river floods, rain batters, and Orual still thinks this is good. She hopes these signs are proof of the rage of some dreadful beast until . . .

A great light comes. Lewis describes it as a lightning that remains, something that illuminates all, and in its midst was the god, the shape of a man of beauty holding still above Orual. She could only look at his face for a moment, for the divine beauty was too great. In a single look, he rejected her yet "denied, answered, and (worst of all) he knew, all I had thought, done, or been" (173). Surely he is more than Cupid in the original myth. Is this god of love like Christ? After all, Orual next says that all her doubt and questions were as nothing before him. In his presence, it's as if she had always known he was real. This moment brings more questions for Orual because if he is real, then her understanding of her past must change.

The god speaks with both sweetness and intensity "like a bird singing on the branch above a hanged man" (173). I wonder if Orual employs such an image because she knows she deserves to die. Does she think she's about to be executed? The god speaks first of Psyche's harsh exile before pronouncing over Orual, "You also shall be Psyche" (174). What does his statement mean? This just might be the greater riddle because the remainder of the novel revolves around that proclamation. Then the light and voice vanish, and Orual is left to hear the weeping of Psyche fade away.

The landscape works against Orual, and she is not able to

follow Psyche. As dawn arrives, the ravaged valley is visible along with dead sheep and deer. Orual makes her way back to poor Gram, who is more than anxious to depart and says even less than before. Interestingly enough, Orual states that she's "proved" that the gods are real and intent on harming her. She did instigate the debacle with Psyche and Cupid, but she never purposed to prove their reality. It had all been about rescuing Psyche and regaining her singular love. How Orual's thoughts have changed! As she and Gram descend, the paranoia of impending death or harm increases. Orual mentions falling off a cliff at any moment or turning into a beast the next. The gods are her executioners. And, if she will be Psyche, Orual literally assumes if she survives, then she will be doomed to exile as well.

Chapter 16
THE VEIL REMAINS

"A treaty with my ugliness"

SLINKING BACK INTO the palace, like a child who knows they have done wrong, Orual realizes she is avoiding the Fox. Poobi takes care of Orual's wound, and the Fox arrives. Grateful to see her again, the Fox expresses his worry and care for her. He is quite surprised that she had returned to the mountain without telling him. Orual hides her wounded arm and is ashamed now of her manipulation of Psyche. But Lewis is careful to describe Orual's shame in the Fox's presence. She is ashamed of what he would think, not of what she had done, not yet.

Eager to hear news of Psyche, the Fox questions Orual. Orual gives a puzzling and circuitous account, beginning with the ravaged state of the valley. She reluctantly admits to speaking with Psyche, but the Fox can tell by her pauses that she is not altogether truthful. Once Orual reveals her plan with the lamp, the Fox is both shocked and distressed. From his viewpoint, the mountain man could have reacted in a number of dangerous ways. Once again, Orual reflects at how clear his reasoning sounds in the light of day away from the mountain. Yet we know she knows the truth of who the "man" was. Why does she even entertain an alternate theory? Oh how Orual wishes her veil was on, implying her need to hide from the truth and from the Fox's need for truth. The Fox wants to know how Orual managed to persuade Psyche to leave the mountain, and all Orual will say is that she did. She cannot tell anything further, which saddens the Fox. He knows she is withholding, but he offers her grace. The Fox does not pressure or manipulate: "my tormenting you to find it would build a worse barrier between us than your hiding it" (180). Orual weeps at this. Surely she is aware of the stark contrast between her manipulation of Psyche and the Fox's love for her.

Once the Fox leaves, Orual knows that she will never tell the truth to Bardia either. Amidst these resolutions, Orual chooses from this moment on to wear her veil, not as a disguise as on her mountain trips or as something forced on her as at her stepmother's wedding, but as something else. She is put to the test within a few days as the King returns from his hunt. Out of sorts as usual, he summons her to the Pillar Room and demands that she remove her "frippery," her "curtains" (181). When she calmly refuses him, the King grows quiet before dismissing her resolve as something all women do. That small defiance changes their relationship. Orual states "he never struck me, and I never feared him again" (182). She now demands freedom from tending Redival too, and the King relinquishes her care to Batta. Apparently, Redival and Batta are equal gossips and cheats. Batta has become a strange ally for the king, filling his mind with gossip and flattery.

As time passes, Orual slowly comes to realize that she "might be doomed to live" (183), that the gods might not kill her yet. With that, she goes to Psyche's room and destroys the evidence, burning Psyche's poetry to the god of the mountain and almost anything of her adult life. I'm again reminded of a courtroom scene. In the last chapter, Orual was a badgering prosecutor. Now she behaves like a dirty policeman, covering for herself. Orual reverts the room and even her memories to Psyche's childhood, keeping only the childish garments and trinkets, a time where Psyche had "belonged" to Orual. What is the nature of Orual's love for Psyche? The door is locked, and so is Orual's mind to this point in time. It is another conscious choice on her part and one more moment of denial. How do you grieve the loss of someone when you don't know whether they're dead or alive?

Orual moves on with her life. She demands hard and deeper knowledge from the Fox and fencing lessons from Bardia, determined to "drive all the woman out of me" (184), to ignore the pain she does feel and to fill herself with doing. But at night when she is alone, Orual sometimes weeps for Psyche, wondering at her hardships and exile. And just as quickly she "rebuilds the dam" that she had set in place, the one that keeps her from feeling, the one that perhaps helps her function.

But something unexpected happens. That winter during feast time, the King is injured in a fall on the palace steps. His thigh is broken and cannot be reset. In considerable agony and with considerable alcohol in him, the Second Priest, the surgeon, and the soldiers have difficulty holding him down. In this frantic state, he raves at Orual who is supervising his care. He wants her gone, apprehensively saying he knows who is behind the veil. We know he isn't speaking of Orual. Who else would come and haunt him? The next day is much the same, and it is clear that the King will not recover.

The leaders of Glome—Bardia, the Fox, Orual, and the Second Priest—unofficially convene, and we are more fully introduced to Arnom, Glome's Second Priest. He is the same age as Orual, dark-skinned and shaven. He announces that the Priest is dying, and all there realize the tenuous position of Glome, as both the King and the Priest are failing. Orual thinks the worst and tells us that there will be a new Glome, and that she will be exiled from leadership. These are only her thoughts. Maybe this calms her. She thinks that now she "shall be a Psyche" (186). Yet within minutes, as the men discuss a needed unity between Ungit and Glome, Bardia declares that there is no issue between the Queen and Ungit. The Fox chimes in, and Arnom is taken aback. What of marriage, what of war? Bardia's quick defense is assuring as Arnom stares at Orual in her veil. Arnom immediately brings up the single issue that divides them, a fertile river area known as the Crumbles. Orual insists that she speaks for the King and drives a fair bargain, freely giving the Crumbles to Arnom and the temple while retaining command of Ungit's guards. In an instant, her new identity has begun, and Bardia whispers "Long live the queen" as the men go to attend the King. Orual, however, can see that this newness will not alter the internal barrier she is still building— "It might strengthen the dam, though" (189). Then she realizes that her father will soon be gone. As the palace quiets for the night, Orual thinks she hears a girl weeping. She follows the sound outside by the well, where she had heard the sound before when the chains moved in the wind. Crying out Psyche's name, she waits and hears nothing until she spots a form moving across the grounds. She races after it and reaches into the bushes to grab a man's hand as he asks for the King.

Chapter 17
THE PRISONER OF PHARS AND THE QUEEN

*"If Orual could vanish altogether into the
Queen, the gods would almost be cheated."*

THROUGH A LIGHT, flirtatious dance of conversation in the moonlight, Orual meets Trunia of Phars. It's quite the introduction. One moment she thought she heard her sister, the next, a complete stranger is telling her how her beautiful voice belies a beautiful face. Once he reveals who he is, Orual must play the politician. She explains to him that she will soon be Queen, and so calling himself a suppliant, Trunia appeals to her for lodging and protection. To remain neutral with Phars, however, Orual cannot. She must take him as prisoner, which he naturally refuses. Within moments, Trunia attempts to run away in the dark, injures his ankle, and returns to her. She calls for guards who bring him into the palace where he is fed.

In class conversations, I often stop the story here and ask my students why Lewis includes Trunia. Some simply say the story at the moment would become boring without him. Others that Orual really is a woman in spite of how others treat her in her ugliness. But why else?

In the meantime, Orual returns to the King's room. His condition had worsened but he watches as Orual, the Fox, and Bardia share news. Trunia's brother Argan and a small force have entered Glome, looking for his brother. Bardia expresses his worry until Orual interrupts with her news. Immediately the Queen, she orders Trunia to be taken to the tower room, where Psyche had been kept, and Orual and her advisors begin to reason through the sticky situation. They logically consider several outcomes to a confrontation. The most critical piece of information is that Argan was hated by many and had once done something contemptible and cowardly. Perhaps this is why Orual next asks Bardia what type of swordsman he was. Her thought is that Argan just might agree to fight against one man to bolster his reputation and eliminate a battle. Diplomatically, Orual's thinking is most advantageous to her, the country, Trunia himself, and the neighboring kingdom. <u>As readers, I think we are all pleasantly surprised at her deft strategy and self-confidence.</u> We haven't met this Orual, and neither have the Fox or Bardia.

The final stroke of genius comes when Orual announces that the best combatant must be one Argan would be loathe to lose to. The men automatically assume the fighter would be a slave, but Orual counters with herself. We aren't surprised, but the men are. Bardia worries about luck overcoming skill, and the Fox cannot believe a woman could do that, for it was "against all custom—all nature—all modesty" (197).

Within these conversations, harsh truths are revealed. Orual tells us that Bardia doesn't think highly of the "word-weaver" Fox, and the Fox thinks Bardia is a barbarian. Yet they must work together. When Orual argues to fight against Argan herself. Bardia passionately agrees that she could fight and fight well, but states "it's a thousand pities they [the gods] didn't make you a man" (197). What a cruel almost ruinous statement, and Orual's thoughts mirror ours here, as if a gallon of cold water were dashed in your broth. Bardia's declaration almost sounds like something King Trom would say. To make matters worse, the Fox lowers himself from his lofty, logical soapbox to true emotional appeal. Pathos and tears reign. Women cannot and should not do this. Psyche is gone, and you leave me, an old man, with nothing. But, Orual presses the men. Like a lawyer once again, she argues that the people would accept her as their ruler if she won. The duel would cement her rule. She forges ahead and states the terms for the fight to be sent by messenger before saying good night.

Alone now, Orual must stop and breathe again. I think even

she was surprised by her behavior and quick thinking. She calls that part of her the Queen, but not Orual. Myriad doubts set in—"Where did the bluff and courage come from moments before? What if I fail? What will people think?" But Orual's doubts go further off course in moments. She next thinks the people might compare her to Psyche if she fails, and within herself, Orual defends and claims a better position, a mental list of her accomplishments, most especially the things Psyche didn't or couldn't do. Orual catches herself of course, thinking she might be a little insane, but it causes us to wonder what is at the root of this competitive stream of thoughts. She is not altogether done. Orual considers whether or not the gods might use this potential fight as a means to kill her, to be rid of her and have their justice.

With that, Orual returns to her father's bedchamber. Terror in his eyes, he is awake but unable to communicate. Orual wonders if he really thought she was Psyche come to murder him. She doesn't delight in his fear but is comforted by the thought that he can no longer control her, alive or dead. Her veil remains, and we wonder when she will use it next.

Chapter 18
KINGS AND PRIESTS

*"but he holds his priesthood permanently,
because he continues forever"* —Hebrews 7:24

THE NEXT MORNING when Orual went to check on the King, she is soon accosted by Redival. Of course, Redival wants to know what will happen to her when the King dies, and at the same time, she must absolutely know who the new handsome man in the house is. Orual is not moved by her emotional banter and severely declares "Your treatment shall be according to your behaviour" (203). Redival immediately reacts by fawning and whining over her sister, hoping for a chance at a husband. It's such a laughable moment, and yet such a quick flash of the new stern Queen.

The Fox arrives next with a genuine apology, "I was wrong to weep and beg and try to force you by your love" (204). But ironically Orual doesn't have a moment to ponder this almost-proverb before Bardia arrives with news of Argan's messenger. After delivering a few insults about having to fight a woman, the messenger relays that Argan will do it, and they take time to lay out the full agreement between the two countries. Arnom soon enters in full priest regalia, and Orual knows the first Priest has died. Yet seeing Arnom in the bird mask doesn't stir her normal fear reaction of Ungit. An interesting note to make. Is she so different as Queen suddenly? Or could she be that much more mature or otherwise changed?

Bardia leads Orual away to discuss both strategy and the reality of killing a man for the first time. Orual is not daunted and even consoles herself, knowing that she was able to stab herself in the arm. Bardia continues and advises her to take part in slaughtering a pig for the day's feast. Apparently, pigs are an abomination to Ungit, but the people may eat them. Orual resolves, "if I shrank from this there would at once be less Queen and more Orual in me" (207). Now we know what she has determined. The part of her that is Orual must diminish, and she is quite conscious of it.

As Queen, she next declares that the Fox is free. Congratulations abound, yet the Fox is stunned after so many years. He must think on it, and suddenly Orual realizes what she has done, "I could not understand the strength of the desire which must be drawing my old master to his own land" (208). She begins to doubt once again, and though she thought the Fox was a "pillar" in her life, Orual is almost sure he will leave her because she had just been his "solace" while imprisoned by her father. Orual's ramble through numerous untruths continue, but by evening the Fox comes to her, announcing that he will remain because he has been gone from his family and homeland too long. What would he return to? Lewis' physical description of the Fox perhaps says even more. His face is grey, he looks as if he had been tortured, and he even says, "I have won a battle" (210). I'm not sure Orual in her rejoicing truly understood what it took for the Fox to choose to remain in Glome.

That night, Orual is riddled with thoughts, sure that the gods were bringing these great changes. Her awareness of the sorrow she always carried for Psyche had waned, which shocked her. It has always been part of Orual, and she thinks, "Orual dies if she ceases to love Psyche" while the queen side of her is more than happy to let Orual go.

The next day crowds assemble and cheer and the lords and elders arrive to wait with the veiled Queen. Orual goes to Trunia and relates the day's plan without mentioning her part in the fight, and somehow the ever-curious Redival arrives with wine for both, playing her part masterfully. Trunia is sufficiently intrigued, to the point that once Redival departs, he offers marriage first to Orual and then to Redival. Orual can hardly believe the proposal, and we realize it is yet one more event the gods seem to have contrived within this short period of time. By evening, Orual is practicing her swordsmanship with Bardia, and he is determined to array her in armor fit for a Queen. They go to the King's bedchamber to sift through what armor there is and find the Fox sitting quietly by the King. Moments after they begin foraging, the Fox announces that the King has died. Bardia and Orual pause and yet resume their search, a most pitiful and truthful display of the unimportant life of an unloved king. Is there a lesson to be learned? Both a king and a priest have passed on.

Chapter 19
A KILLING MATTER

*"It was the strangest thing in the world
to look upon him, a man like any other man,
and think that one of us presently would kill the other."*

WHAT DOES A great fight look like? As Queen, Orual soon realizes the preparation is extensive and exasperating. The Fox should appear in formal dress, but he won't. Bardia wants her to go veilless, but she won't. Poobi must sew a special veil to fit over the helmet. Ghostlike in appearance, Orual appears daunting according to Bardia. And soon enough, this proves true when Trunia emerged to join the procession. He is startled by her, too.

As the city elders join them, the royal procession leaves the gates of the palace, and Orual does recognize the ironic parallel to Psyche's life. So too, Psyche had left the gates to heal the people and later to appease the people with her sacrifice. Naturally, Orual wonders if this is how she fulfills the god's words. Is this how they will be the same?

Maybe we can take a moment here to consider now how often Lewis utilizes irony. From the moment of Psyche's birth, itself an irony since she is one more girl, to the fact that the Fox was hired to teach a prince, the tool of irony is quite clear. The Fox never does teach a prince, but he does foster a queen and becomes a trusted advisor. I'm sure the King never intended it, but he most definitely benefited from it. What other ironies will we see?

As Orual nears the field, the people stupidly cheer. She knows they are just eager for entertainment. They care not if she wins. Arnom appears in his bird mask, and a sacrifice must be made before the fight. Orual and Argan must each eat a morsel of bull flesh and make the proper vows before the people. The crowds are pushed back, Bardia and Argan's man make the final agreements, and the trumpets must sound as the fight begins. Trunia is stunned when he sees Orual remove her cloak and stride out to face Argan while the Fox remains stoic. Orual quickly measures Argan's disrespect as they begin. To her, the fight was exactly like all of her practice matches with Bardia and appears unchallenging: "I did not believe in the combat at all" (219). Argan soon recognizes how fairly matched they are, and worry sets in. The reality of death has arrived. After a second mistake, Orual took her opening and sliced Argan's inner thigh and likely the femoral artery. No ancient surgeon could repair such a wound, and all present know it's a death blow. Through much cheering, <u>Orual recognizes this death at her hands has already changed her permanently, much like the loss of virginity</u>. Bardia, the Fox, and Trunia surround her with praise, and Orual weeps behind the veil for a moment. But she must address the people and quickly mounts a horse beside Trunia to address the lords and soldiers of Phars. Most of the men shout for Trunia, and the rest gallop away. Trunia's succession is secure, and she must provide a feast among men when she'd much rather celebrate with an intimate few. Surprisingly, Trunia continues to praise and even flirt with Orual, who very much enjoys the attention and flattery. She realizes that she feels happy for once, but at the same time, knows that the gods won't let it last, "...the gods' old trick; blow the bubble up big before you prick it" (222). Almost immediately word comes that Bardia's wife is in labor, and he is needed at home. Bardia asks Orual for permission to leave, but it's how he asks for permission that disturbs her most, "the day's work is over" (222). Though she maintains her composure in the moment with a blessing to him, Orual is dismayed and discouraged that this powerful and weighty occasion, a crucial moment for her and for Glome, is just work.

    As Orual hosts the celebratory banquet, she is simultaneously disgusted and pleased by the men's attention. But this is not the place for her. She leaves the drunken mess, but drunk herself, reveals to us one of her strongest imaginations, that of Bardia as her husband and Psyche as her daughter. In one way, we understand that this is how Orual wants to relate to both, yet we know this is her fiction, much like an actor. She feels a "glorious and noble sorrow" for her losses, and her inebriated mind plays a pitiful chorus as she falls asleep with the most final of words, "I am the Queen; I'll kill Orual too" (225).

Chapter 20
A QUEEN'S REIGN

*"And I applied my heart to know wisdom
and to know madness and folly. I perceived that
this also is a striving after wind."* —Ecclesiastes 1:17

AND SHE ALMOST does. Orual locks that part of herself away like a reverse pregnancy, and the Queen part of herself gains dominance. As in her introduction in the first chapter, the Queen remains: "I was Orual the eldest daughter of Trom, King of Glome" (4). Her new identity, though, is her choice. No advisor demands this change.

As years pass, the legend of the Queen evolves. From her fight with Argan to the one battle where she slays seven in a fury to save Bardia, the Queen is famous. In her narrative to us, she is quick to correct and downplay the weave of growing stories. False humility or not, the Queen attributes much of her success to her wise advisors, the Fox and Bardia. Fortunately, neither cares about power and so each gives neutral and balanced advice. Here, Lewis does say that "they did not think of me as a woman" (228). Why this diminishing of her femininity? Bardia had already trained her as a man, a soldier, to ease her mind from the loss of Psyche, yet this treatment somehow remains. Orual even thinks the gods see women as lesser. By chapter's end, she writes, <u>"The one sin the gods never forgive us is that of being born women"</u> (233).

Her second point is that the veil added to the mystery and the strength of her reign. It sparked incredible rumors. Some said the veil hid an animal face, others an emptiness, and still others dazzling beauty. The Queen even uses it to her benefit in trade and politics to inspire fear and anxiety in the leaders who come to treat with her. Whatever the veil means to others, Orual still hides herself behind it. Remember that Orual first wore a veil in Chapter 1 as a child because the Priest demanded it at her father's wedding. It is not a wedding veil, a symbol of innocence and parental covering. It is no longer a funeral veil, to hide mourning and create a separation of privacy. No, these are seasons in life, while Orual's veil is permanent. Paul speaks of a permanent veil, a veil of choice, in II Corinthians 3:14-15: *What is more, their minds were made stonelike; for to this day the same veil remains over them when they read the Old Covenant; it has not been unveiled, because only by the Messiah is the veil taken away. Yes, till today, whenever Moshe is read, a veil lies over their heart.* (CJB)

I think we could agree that there is a veil over Orual's heart too, a natural barrier to block grief or the wounds of being mostly unloved. The question is whether the veil will ever be lifted or removed or by whom. The Queen next speaks of moving her quarters in the palace to the north to be away from the clanking chains of the well, the ones that remind her of Psyche weeping. But her sister is not forgotten. She admits to employing servants to track every rumor and trace of Psyche to no avail.

What follows in Chapter 20 is indeed a list of accomplishments. Batta is hanged. Slaves are sold off, and some are freed to marry and work the land of Glome, including Poobi. The silver mines are improved upon, the men treated fairly, profit soars. The Fox is given an ample apartment and monies to purchase books, all eighteen in the royal library! The Queen develops relationships with her nobles, and even Bardia's wife Ansit. Ansit is a typical woman in Glome, no longer beautiful, and quite large after bearing eight children. Our Queen is underwhelmed by what might be in her mind the competition, yet she tries to treat Ansit well. She thinks of all that Ansit shares with Bardia, all the womanly attributes, and then in her mind contrasts those with what she has had with Bardia, all the manly duties. Somehow, the Queen makes herself appear superior. But is she?

What exactly is she justifying? Here, I usually remind my students that Orual is the narrator. It is her book and perspective always.

There are improvements in Glome's religion too. Arnom renovates the temple, opening it to light and air, and brings in a new statue that resembles a woman as they do in Greece. The Queen comments that the darkness and holy smell or reek of the temple has dissipated. She admits that "an image of this sort would somehow be a defeat for the old, hungry, faceless Ungit whose terror had been over me in childhood" (234). So, now Ungit has a face in one form and remains shapeless in the other as the two stones stand together in the temple. What does this portend for Orual? Does she not have two aspects as well?

In his old age, the Fox writes a history of Glome and begins to call the Queen by more than one boy's name. Perhaps he is thinking of his own brothers or children. The Queen continues to fill her hands with doing, and her list begins to sound like Ecclesiastes 2 or the myth of Sisyphus, the story of endless toil, the man who tricked the gods so much he was condemned to eternally roll a boulder up a hill in Hades. Laws are rewritten, the Shennit river is deepened for trade, water is stored, and so on. She says, "I did and I did and I did—and what does it matter what I did?" (236). It is a conscious busyness that could not fill her as time passes relentlessly. And so, the Fox dies and is buried, while the Queen's reign slogs on. She finally decides to sojourn to other lands and brings along Bardia's son, Poobi's daughter, and other needed servants and soldiers.

Chapter 21
JOURNEY

"Now, you who read, judge between the gods and me."

THE ONLY REASON Orual even tells us of this journey is because of what happened at the end of it. The journey itself takes place at harvest season or what we would call early autumn, the end of a season of growth which is symbolic for Orual. But first, she relates the visit to Phars where Trunia and Redival rule. Like all women of Glome, Redival is now fat, and true to her nature, ever talkative. Trunia and Orual ignore her and speak together, and we find out that Trunia's second son, Daaran, will assume her throne. Sadly, Orual mentions that she would love Daaran, but she has vowed not to love "any young creature" again, even after all these decades have passed. It is amazing to me that she has lived so long without giving or receiving love, as if love is something dangerous to avoid.

    The group then travels through the mountains and forests of Essur, which neighbors Phars. After a brief visit of three days with the King, they journey to a hot springs instead of going home. Lewis spends some time here describing the autumnal season, "...the sunlight on the stubble looked aged and gentle, not fierce like the summer heats. You would think the year was resting, its work done. And I whispered to myself that I too would begin to rest" (239). Orual's peaceful reflection seems genuine. Her reign is nearing its natural end, the harvest has been gathered, and she feels at rest. In myth and literature, this symbolism of the season is universal and is known as an archetype. Lewis employs it masterfully as Orual's expectations are soon shattered.

    As the young ones build camp, Orual wanders into the depths

of the cool forest after hearing a temple bell sound. She's drawn to a small white pillared temple in a clearing. All is clean, uncluttered, practically pure, a sure contrast to her prior experiences. Within the temple, a small two-foot statue of a woman is swathed in black about the face, "much like my own veil," she relates, "but that mine was white" (241). A simple, black-robed priest walks in and greets her as Orual offers a few coins. Within minutes, the priest recounts the tale of this newer goddess Istra. Remember that Psyche too was named Istra at birth and then gradually became known by the Greek name Psyche. Orual isn't fazed by the name as it is apparently common in Essur. By the priest's tale, Istra was first mortal and was the youngest of three daughters born to a king and queen. As he discloses the full story by memory, Orual is struck by the similarity to her life and interrupts him to ask where he has learned of it. He simply answers that it is the "sacred story" and narrates that the two sisters saw the palace, as in the original myth. Orual is stupefied. She interrupts and counters that it is not true. He states that "they weren't blind" (243). Orual's struggle with the gods and her struggle with doubt forcefully re-emerge from the walls she had built! She blusters and fusses and defends her perspective—no fool could have come up with the priest's version. What are the gods up to? She quickly returns to her accusation, "Do I not do well to write a book against them, telling what they have kept hidden?" (243). If in fact, the sisters had seen the palace, then there would be no riddle and "no guessing wrong." It's as if the defensive veil she wears is being ripped away. The priest said she is not blind, she has seen. "And now to tell my story as if I had had the very sight they had denied me…" (244). Orual's very words reveal so much to us. <u>They denied her. The gods had done this, not her. In her telling, she has removed the choice she had and sounds fatalistic.</u>

But the priest is not done. He next explains how the sisters were jealous of Istra "because they had seen the palace" and all she had (244). Orual explodes again. She realizes she had become like Bardia over the years—leaving the gods alone so that they leave you alone. It had never meant that the gods weren't there or weren't acting. Orual had withdrawn herself, not them. She must write her case against them!

The priest speaks now of Psyche wandering and weeping, of how Talapal (Essur's Ungit) sets difficult tasks for her to complete, of how Psyche is successful and reunited with her husband to become a goddess. To symbolize this momentous change, the black veil on the temple statue is completely removed in the spring and summer. So then, can this Istra, this Psyche see? Isn't Orual to be Psyche as the god said? These are descriptions of hope for the doubt-full and antagonistic Orual, but she chooses not to see. She argues with the priest that the sisters would have more to say and abruptly leaves. It is now dark, and she makes her way back to the camp, thinking of the feelings she is hiding and of how she must write her accusation, her defense—"I was with book, as a woman is with child" (247).

Though the return journey relays scene after scene of bounty and goodness through Essur and Glome, Orual has removed her inner walls and begins to relive the "terrors, humiliations, struggles, and anguish...letting Orual wake and speak, digging her almost out of a grave, out of the walled well" (247). She urges and forces her companions to quicken their pace and refrains from talking with them. Her sudden and morose behaviour change affects them all.

Once home in Glome (or is it gloom?), Orual is dismayed by the work awaiting her and annoyed that Bardia is ill. She is sure his wife is just keeping him home from her and the palace intentionally. Nevertheless, she finishes her book and finally and clearly spells out her purpose for us in writing:

> "Now, you who read, judge between the gods and me. They gave me nothing in the world to love but Psyche and then took her from me but that was not enough...they would not tell me whether she was

the bride of a god, or mad, or a brute's or villain's spoil. They would give no clear sign...and because I guessed wrong they punished me...through her" (249).

Isn't it interesting that she asks us to judge what is true? She has shared these exclusive and limited parts of her life with us. She has told us her story in all subjectivity, and yet calls on us as if we could be neutral as a jury. But can we? Another point to consider is that the name Orual closely resembles the Greek word for *pickaxe*. After reading all that Orual has tried to make sense of, she is still mining, still "picking" for that the valuable gem of truth.

At this point, almost all of Orual's theology emerges in the chapter. Orual is sure the gods have created this lying story throughout the world like the one the priest told with the idea that there had never been a riddle, that she had always been able to see, and that she was jealous. According to her, the gods are manipulative and mean and never clear. They give dreams and visions and hints and whispers as if in a game. "Why must holy places be dark places?" (249) she queries once again. Orual ends defiantly—let the gods do what they will, then everyone will know who they are and that they have no answer.

PART II

Chapter 1
A RIP IN THE VEIL

*"Those divine Surgeons had
me tied down and were at work."*

ORUAL FUSSES THAT she must add more to her book even though she has finished. The writing process itself has taught her much. What she thought she remembered had awakened even more "passions and thoughts." What's more, "The change which the writing wrought in me (and of which I did not write) was only a beginning—only to prepare me for the gods' surgery" (254). What an interesting phrase! We will soon find out what "gods' surgery" is. As she wrote the beginning of this very book, something interrupted her work—an embassy from the Great King arrived at the palace. The eunuch leader of this entourage was large and gaudy and yet at the feast she held, Orual knew something was familiar about him. She suddenly shouted out, "Tarin!" and he responded that her father may not have loved him but becoming a eunuch made him a successful man. Though he repeatedly makes fun of the tiny country of Glome, Tarin recounts his time with Redival and reveals that Redival felt lonely and unloved. This is the first time Orual even thinks of how life might have been for Redival. Before, she only thought of herself, Psyche, and the Fox. She had always assumed the golden-haired and pretty Redival had an easier life than herself. This is but the first small tear in the veil of Orual's defenses.

Orual continues writing and choosing what to write about, so much so that the process bleeds over into her sleep and her dreams begin. In her dream, she is endlessly sorting piles of seeds and grains, as if she could not determine what to include in her book. In the original myth, Venus gave Psyche this impossible task because it was impossible and to keep her from Cupid, the one she loved. But in the myth, it was no dream, which makes us wonder how it fully applies to Orual's waking life. Remember that the god of the Grey Mountain said, "You also shall be Psyche." And so Lewis has drawn in another parallel from the myth. Yet Orual dreams of this over and over, sometimes dreaming of herself as an ant, vainly trying to lift a single seed when there are thousands.

Her nights and days are full of these thoughts and memories and writing, and somehow she neglects to ask after Bardia until Arnom appears on the very day she finishes. Orual suddenly understands his news that Bardia has been ill for some time and is too weary to fight it. Arnom wisely cautions her not to go to him because then Bardia would feel obligated to rise and be of service. Orual waits in agony. Five days later Bardia dies. Though she knows it would have embarrassed and shamed him, Orual regrets that she never told him she loved him.

Days later at Bardia's funeral pyre, Orual cannot weep or cry out, for only family is allowed to. Her pain is great. She later visits his widow Ansit, who receives her formally while Orual makes a gracious condolence speech. It is a stiff and awkward meeting, yet as the exchange continues, Ansit quickly turns blunt and unforgiving. She reveals that Bardia was not strong but "a tree that is eaten away within" (260). He had been overworked and over loyal for years. Ansit accuses Orual indirectly of overworking Bardia in the Pillar Room, just like any man in the mines. If only she had known, Orual states. But Ansit plunges on, saying that loyal and loving servants like Bardia surround the Queen. Orual is sure, though, that no one would begrudge her that type of love and loyalty since that is all she has without a husband or children. As her feelings escalate, Ansit lashes out that Orual left her "her share" of Bardia because he had been so used up by Orual. Orual is stunned and accuses Ansit of being jealous of her. At the same time, she pulls aside her veil as if seeing her ugly visage could persuade Ansit. Instead, Ansit sees the mix of genuine grief and love Orual had for Bardia. This time, Ansit is stunned and brought to tears. They weep together for a brief moment before the argument renews. Orual wonders why Ansit didn't stop her reliance on Bardia before while Ansit explains that that in itself would have removed Bardia's choice in the matter. To worsen the situation, Orual now has "taken" their firstborn Ilerdia, and Ansit knows she will little see and know him as he serves the palace too.

But perhaps the most grinding and piercing truth comes next. <u>Ansit repudiates Orual for not understanding love</u>. She implies that true love let's go and does not control. Maybe hers is unique and not like the rest of mankind: "Perhaps you who spring from the gods love like the gods. Like the Shadowbrute. <u>They say the loving and the devouring</u> are all the same, don't they?" (265). <u>What? Orual is like the very gods she accuses?</u> What a cruel twist for Ansit to employ these words. She adds that Orual, however, has "fed" and "gorged" herself on the lives of others—Bardia, Ansit, the Fox, Redival, Psyche. Filled with anger, Orual leaves the room without harming her, though she definitely entertained the idea of torture and death for Ansit.

And now we return to the gods' surgery that Orual first introduced at the beginning of this chapter. The truth of all that Ansit said is laid open before Orual. She cannot deny it or hide any longer. Even her idea of love for him proves empty and "the craving for Bardia was ended" (267). <u>Metaphor though it is, the gods have made the incision and are probing her, causing her to look at herself instead of others. Her bookwriting, her dreams, and Ansit's words have been their instruments.</u>

Chapter 2
WHAT VEIL?

*"The voice of the god had not
changed in all those years, but I had"*

IT IS SPRINGTIME, and Glome celebrates the new year. The Priest remains in Ungit's temple overnight before bursting forth and symbolically fighting with someone as a sign that the new year has departed from the West (often an archetype for death or winter) to emerge in the East (representing life and spring). As a virgin still, Orual was not allowed to be part of the overnight rituals as a King would be. Lewis describes drinking, sacrifice, and intercourse with the temple girls. Orual, however, arrives in the morning in the temple with the same lifelong visceral reaction to its smells and "smothering" (269). As she sits in her designated spot by the original Ungit, she reflects on all the seed that had been spilled and wasted on these temple girls in service of Ungit. All that had been "given" to Ungit was fruitless and wasted, much like Orual's own life of accomplishments. She stares at the shapeless blob and indeed sees faces in spite of the fact that the rock appeared faceless. Again, another irony considering the title of the book. Orual asks Arnom, "Who is Ungit?" (270). This time, rather than a circuitous answer as the first Priest would have offered, Arnom replies in a rather general way: "She signifies the earth, which is the womb and mother of all living things" (270). She sounds like a caregiver, a nurturer, not the frightening thing Orual has experienced. What's even more interesting is that Orual had just recounted for us, her audience, the original, more primitive story right before inquiring of Arnom. She tells us, the stone of Ungit had not fallen from the sky, but had pushed up from the earth. That statement will help us understand Orual's imminent dreams.

As Orual questions Arnom about what Ungit has made, his answers simply beg more questions. She's convinced the riddle of the gods remains. Who can understand? Apparently, no one.

A penitent old woman comes in to offer a pigeon as sacrifice. Once the blood is spilled over the stone, she weeps prostrate for awhile but then rises calmly. Orual asks her why she sacrifices to the large stone rather than the new, womanlike statue, and the woman explains that the Greek type statue is only for learned and high-ranking people. The amorphous stone is much simpler and understands her. What does Lewis mean here? Could he be saying that the common people cherish a simpler, less legalistic religion? Is the old better than the new?

The spring ritual continues, and Orual is amazed by the ignorant joy of the people as they witness this sham fight with Arnom emerging from the temple. Again, what could Lewis be saying about the humble faith of the people? Orual soon returns to the palace to rest in her quarters when she is startled by her father's voice. Lewis doesn't clarify if Orual actually laid down or even fell asleep. I tend to think this is the beginning of a waking vision. The King commands her to rise and follow him to the Pillar Room without the veil, "None of that folly" (274), and she does. Her self-imposed barrier is gone. Orual is fearful that the King will want his treasured mirror she had given to Redival—or maybe she would be fearful to stand in front of it now without her veil after all these years. They suddenly find two pickaxes (remember her name meaning) and a crowbar in the corner of the Pillar Room and get to work removing a portion of the floor at the King's direction. Soon enough, a sizable hole is made, and they jump down and fall into a second, smaller Pillar Room made of earth. It's not claustrophobic yet, and we are reminded of Ungit's emergence from the womb of the earth although they are going deeper. The King finds two spades in the corner and commands Orual to dig again. It is harder this time as they dig out blocks of clay, but they make a hole and the King commands her to jump with him again. Though she resists, the King shouts that the Fox and his thinking can't reach her here. Isn't that true of a dream? Your thinking cannot get in the way of the experience or truth of the dream itself.

They land in an even smaller Pillar Room made of "living rock" and the roof begins to close in on them. Orual grows alarmed and claustrophobic. She uses the word "smothering" again as she did when describing the sensation that arises when she enters Ungit's temple. The King then demands, "Who is Ungit?" and leads her down a hallway to the mirror. Didn't she just ask that same question of Arnom? She resists, but he stands her in front of it. Orual sees the King's reflection and then her own, which is now the blob of face from the stone in the temple. He asks her again, and Orual wails, "I am Ungit!" (276) and immediately wakens.

Orual knows it is true, for she had devoured people as Ansit said, "womblike, yet barren" (276). In that instant of recognition, her instinct is to draw her old sword from the wall and kill herself, yet Orual does not have the strength. She feels sure that there must "be something great in the mortal soul" because her suffering, man's suffering, seems unending (277).

Time and days pass. One night once the palace was sleeping, Orual put on her cloak and removed her veil to walk through the city. She knows now that the veil cannot keep her hidden, for all people know the veiled Queen: "My disguise now would be to go bareface" (278). In her old and wrinkled body, Orual is unafraid to be seen. She tells us that she is Ungit in all her ugliness, she is holy now. Yet, the irony remains that she is walking about in the dark when no one is looking at her. That to me is symbolic in itself. Is she still walking in the dark here at the end of life? She has lived a life of doubt, fearing to believe in something she can't see. I wonder if she still is thinking literally. Orual has removed her veil and even mentions going out buff-naked. This is her external or physical "ugliness." What of the internal?

Though she wearies quickly, Orual makes her way to a high bank of the Shennit River, intending to drown herself. She removes her girdle, which is a cloth belt, and uses it to tie her ankles together. When she hops almost to the edge, Orual hears a voice cry out, "Do not do it" (279). It is the voice of a god, one she knows, one she has heard from across a river before at the top of the Grey Mountain. Like Saul on his way to Damascus, she exclaims, "Lord, who are you?" (279). He responds that she cannot escape Ungit (or is it being Ungit?) through death. Instead, the god's voice says "Die before you die" (279). Not only does Orual immediately acknowledge he is who he is by calling him "Lord," but she also knows she has changed within. "No rebel" is left. Does that mean her internal veil, that thing that stands in the way of full belief, is now gone? And what of the words that echo Christ's? To die before you die. In the gospels, Jesus repeatedly speaks of laying down his life for his sheep, a choice he makes before he is ever crucified. At the same time, he admonishes his disciples to deny themselves, their selfish human natures, and to take up their crosses, their burdens, as they follow Jesus (Matthew 16:24). Isn't this the denial and death of our inner nature? When Jesus spoke to the Samaritan woman at the well and explained who he was in John 11:25, he said, I am the *resurrection and the life. Whoever believes in me, though he die, yet shall he live.* To the Samaritan women, this must have sounded like a riddle. To Orual, to die before you die meant to stay alive. She knew with everything within her she was not to kill herself. The god's voice, the hearing of it, brought clarity, and Orual hobbles back to the palace in the cover of night.

Chapter 3
THE COMPLAINT

"But," says the Torah, "whenever someone turns to ADONAI, *the veil is taken away."* —II Corinthians 3:16 (CJB)

IN THE LAST chapter, Orual removed both her outer veil and her inner one. Through her time in the temple, her vision involving the king, and her suicide attempt, her understanding of herself and the god has increased. Notice that Lewis no longer refers to *the gods* plurally but has instead returned to include *the one* Orual knows. Yes, he is Cupid in the original myth, but more importantly, he is the god of love, and Orual knows his voice. Jesus said that his sheep know his voice and won't follow the voice of a stranger, and what's more, he calls them by name (John 10:2-5). This personal god knows her.

As Orual reflects on the words of the god, she is reminded of both the Fox's words and those of Socrates. If Socrates said that true wisdom is the skill and practice of death, then Orual realizes that passions and opinions will fall away and die. Now she thinks she understands the words of her father in the dream. "I am Ungit" means she must stop "devouring" and being ugly from the inside. Orual vows to be upright and virtuous each day. Surely the gods will help! Yet they don't, and Orual falls into old behaviors and patterns without success. She cannot be virtuous on her own. Whose voice is she listening to now? Perhaps Lewis is highlighting our frail humanness or even the weakness of humanism. How can we live well if we rely on ourselves only?

Orual is sure the gods are not helping and will not help her. After all, she has no physical nor inner beauty. It seems that each person is fated from birth to be beautiful in some way, and she is not. Therefore, they will not help her. As Lewis brings in this idea of fatalism, he identifies one more human means of coping in life. We should not turn to ourselves and our strengths to live life as humanism espouses, and neither should we blame fate, as if we have no choice. Orual cannot see that she has always had choice. She assures us that it is her bitter fate or destiny to be ugly in every way. She queries what if "we were made to be dregs and refuse everywhere and everyway?" (283). Her hopelessness seems absolute but for another dream.

As she walks into her room for an afternoon rest, Orual walks into the next dream. She faces a great river, and across from it, the gods' land, a brilliantly colored scene of green meadow, blue sky, and a flock of enormous golden rams. Orual immediately ventures across the river to get some gold wool because then she thinks she would have beauty. But as she emerges from the water, the flock, like "a wall of living gold," stampedes her, yet she is not injured or dead. Unlike the original myth, Orual's task isn't a physical one designed by Venus. It appears to be a spiritual one. Orual explains that the rams did not trample her in rage but in joy, like a force of the Divine Nature. So has Orual now died before she dies? The question remains.

Within moments in the dream, Orual sees another woman gleaning gold wool from the bushes. How easy for her! Orual reveals much in her next thought: "What I had sought in vain by meeting the joyous and terrible brutes, she took at her leisure. She won without effort what utmost effort would not win for me" (284). Remember "simple Psyche"? Psyche had complete faith and trust in the god of the Grey Mountain, and once she was "sacrificed" by the people of Glome, she was then rescued by Zephyr, carried to the god, and loved by him wholly. Psyche represents all that is faith while Orual still portrays doubt, in that she still must accomplish things the hard way.

Though Lewis doesn't say, Orual must have woken at this point, for she tells us how she goes about her life and work, even meting out the best and wisest rulings ever when her people come to her for justice. She doesn't care about these, however, and comforts herself by reading her own version of how she loved Psyche, the book we are reading.

Next, Orual walks into another vision. This one is harsher. She finds herself toiling through a desert, carrying an empty bowl to gather the waters of death as a gift to Ungit. In the scorching heat and blinding sun, Orual feels as if a hundred years has passed. The unending toil reminds us of more than one Greek myth where the gods have punished mortals with futility. In other cultures, a bowl of water is given to one dying so that they may see their reflection and know themselves before death arrives. We already knew that Orual was near the end of her life, but an empty bowl could be symbolic of the emptiness within Orual.

Her desert journey ends as she arrives at a great almost nightmarish mountain. She knows the well of death she seeks is inside. The brilliant light of the sun remains all about her, and she falls to her knees outside. An eagle lands in front of her, asking who she is and what she carries. He does not care that she is Queen of Glome. Orual looks down at the bowl she has carried across the desert and finds that it is now her scroll. Surely, as the water of death would reflect who she really is, this scroll is all that she is. The eagle announces that she has come with a complaint against the gods. Orual is surrounded quickly by a crowd of things "like men" that push and pull her inside to a waiting crowd. All the time, shouts of "Bring her in!" echo inside and out. Orual is taken from the hot sunlight to the dark recesses of the mountain.

Generally in literature and scripture, moving from light to dark foreshadows evil to come. Yet, remember Orual's visit to the first mountain. It is where she encountered the strongest love. Psyche chose to abandon her god and husband to save Orual, and she did. And here, Orual undeniably heard and saw the god for the first time. Now, she is within the mountain. I'm reminded of Arnom's story of Ungit emerging from her womb of the earth in the springtime. Is this a symbolic, spiritual womb for Orual? A place of birth before her death?

She is pushed by the masses to a platform. All becomes dark and silent before a grey light emerges. In the half-light like the twilight of the gods, Orual can see now tens of thousands of faces, including the ghosts of her father, Bardia, and the Fox. The court was full. Veiled in black, the judge commands Orual to be stripped, and she stands old and naked before them all. As she looks at her scroll, it too appears old and shabby. <u>Again, I think this book, that scroll, represents all she is</u>. They are synonymous. The judge commands her to read the complaint.

As Orual unrolls it and looks at her writing, all she sees is a "vile scribble," as if her writing were some immature emotional graffiti, and soon Orual says, "I heard myself reading" (290). Such a simple sentence, but it is critical. Now Orual finally hears herself make the complaint. The question is what is the complaint?

Orual begins with acknowledging that she did meet a real god and did see his house. She argues that if all gods were like that, real and not hidden like Ungit, then she could have borne their presence. But the gods like Ungit and the Shadowbrute are ugly and cannot be seen as they are wrapped in storied legend. She confronts the gods, exclaiming that stories like the Brute devouring the sacrifice are so obscure, how can they be real? How can you have faith in something like that? <u>Of course, she is unable to see that she too was a devourer</u>.

Orual next asks why the gods stole Psyche's love from her. She doesn't say they stole Psyche herself, not yet. Yes, we can see her jealousy, but it's more than revealing that the loss of love is so impactful. Consider her life and loss. Orual never had a mother. The only nurturing relationship she had was the grandfatherly one with the Fox. Her father was a true abuser, and no man ever loved her for herself. Only Psyche saw Orual for who she was and chose to love her. So of course, the gods torture Orual with the loss of Psyche's love.

More so, Orual adds that the gods not only use their beauty to entice, but they also take the most beautiful from us. She's convinced that beauty is a key likely because it is something she has never had. "You're a tree in whose shadow we can't thrive" (291). Man is always lesser in this competition, and more than once, Orual declares that Psyche was "Mine!" Orual has lost, and she sounds like the poorest of losers.

The judge interrupts her rant, and Orual suddenly knows that she has been reading her complaint over and over and over. A long silence follows. The judge asks her if she received her answer, and Orual says "Yes." She had asked earlier, "How could I want to know it?" or how could she desire to know and acknowledge the gods' existence when Psyche's love was stolen? It needed to be fair, to make sense, and it doesn't. For some reason, Orual still cannot see that Psyche had a choice and that choice was hers only, even though it affected Orual in a monumental way.

Chapter 4
PERFECT LOVE

Now, ADONAI in this text means the Spirit.
And where the Spirit of ADONAI is, there is freedom.
So all of us, with faces unveiled, see as in a mirror the glory of the
Lord; and we are being changed into his very image, from one
degree of glory to the next, by ADONAI the Spirit.
—II Corinthians 3:17-18 (CJB)

THE DREAM CONTINUES. Orual now knows that "the complaint was the answer" because those were the truest words from within her, the words that had been the center of her life, even controlling her life. With these expressed words, Orual can say that nothing stands between her and the gods any longer: "How can they meet us face to face till we have faces?" (294). This is such a complicated thought for my students that I always ask them to paraphrase this question, especially in light of what Lewis may mean as a Christian in relation to God. We could say, "How can God meet with me, be with me, until I know who I am, until I know who I am in Him?"

Immediately, the Fox speaks out and confesses to the judge that he had taught Orual wrongly. The lament that follows is indeed a prolonged confession. He bemoans the fact that he knew the people "got" something from worshipping Ungit. He implies that their simple faith was in fact real in addition to the sacrifices the Priest knew were needed. The gods "will have sacrifice—will have man" (295). I know that sounds barbaric and pagan, but in the Christian sense, the Fox is explaining that God will have us, all of us. He is more disturbed, however, with his deception and confesses that he had fed Orual on words. His Greek wisdom, logic, knowledge—all had failed her and him.

The judge then releases Orual because she had made her accusation and been answered. There was nothing else for her to say or do. She gazes down from the platform, choosing to "end it," flinging herself down to the cave floor. But suicide is not possible here, and somehow the Fox catches her. Orual is astonished at how real and warm he is in this afterlife of a dream. The Fox in turn begs her forgiveness for all the drivel he taught her, yet Orual pleads for his mercy for how she "took" his life. She knows he remained in Glome out of love, and yes, pity for her. He acknowledges that he knew that, but now it's time to go to the true judges. They must answer her complaint.

The Fox leads Orual away from the dark mountain cavern to a special three-walled chamber to wait for her summons by the judges. Filtered sunshine flows into the space from a fourth wall of vines and pillars that lead out into green meadow and shining water. The desert is no more, but could this be the water of death Orual was to gather?

The Fox then serves as guide to the living murals, movies even, that cover the three walls. The first captures the image of a woman walking to the river's edge and then binding her feet with her belt. Surely this is Orual. But no, Orual looks and recognizes Psyche in all her beauty. Remember that Orual feels that beauty is the one thing the gods chose to keep from her. We also remember that the god of the Grey Mountain told Orual she too would be Psyche.

They move to the next picture as it comes to life. This portrays a dim image of Psyche in rags and chains, sorting seeds with the utmost concentration as a swarm of ants aid her in her task. Orual marvels, and they watch a third image of Psyche gathering the gold wool from the gods' rams. It is the same as Orual's waking vision in the previous chapter but without Orual.

The next scene is also familiar. Orual sees herself as a shadow next to Psyche as they toil through the desert. Psyche carries her empty bowl while Orual hugs her scroll. Somehow

TILL WE HAVE FACES: A MYTH RETOLD

Psyche is tired yet happy, singing as she makes her way, "merry and good in heart" (300). As Psyche arrives at the mountain, the eagle takes her bowl and returns it full of the water of death. This alone might imply that Psyche actually is already dead, if she had indeed been given the water and tasted it. At the same time, Orual's shadow disappeared.

Again, Orual is staggered by Psyche's contentment and joy through every trial. How could she be happy? The Fox explains that someone else bore her anguish, and it was Orual. Orual is stunned. He reminds her that the gods and men are all part of each other, thus Orual carried the burden and hardship of Psyche's "impossible" tasks. So reminiscent of I John 3:16, it almost seems as if Orual not only carried her sister's burden but also carried the burden of ugliness. Has she like Jesus given her life for Psyche? That is difficult to answer. The Fox queries whether she "would have rather had justice." And of course Orual says no. As a queen, a ruler of men, she knows how men behave including herself. She makes reference again to the selfish nature of Batta and Redival and herself. She doesn't need justice anymore.

They turn to the third and final wall where Psyche is descending to Hades for the final impossible task of retrieving a box of beauty from Persephone as a gift to Ungit or Venus. Unlike the original myth, there is no deceit involved in Psyche's ordeal. Ungit has not placed a deadly sleep within this casket. Psyche must never speak to a soul as part of the test, and the Fox's narration is strangely reminiscent of the first Priest's style and resembles myth more than fact. Yet in these words, logic is laid aside as the Fox relays how Ungit is within each of us and we must bear her son and die in childbirth or change ourselves. In other words, we must surrender all that we are, and in Orual's case, all of our ugliness, in order to become beautiful. It might sound mythic, yet it is a beautiful metamorphosis. *And whoever does not take his cross and follow me is not worthy of me. Whoever finds his life will lose it, and whoever loses his life for my sake will find it.* Matthew 10:38-39 (ESV)

As Psyche journeys, she walks through myriad temptations. Crowds like those outside the palace walls once called to her for healing cheer her once again, demanding to worship her. Surprisingly, the Fox appears next in the scene, tempting Psyche to disbelieve and remember Greek wisdom. Next comes a shadowy woman who pleads passionately to Psyche to turn aside and come with her. The mysterious figure drips blood from her arm, and Orual knows it is herself. Without her veil, both the real and the symbolic, Orual can now see what she did to Psyche and how she caused her sister anguish. The Fox too acknowledges that together they were Psyche's enemies.

In the most poetic language, the Fox, that is Lewis, next details how mankind will someday be able to truly see how beautiful the gods are. And, more and more people will come to see! "Nothing is yet in its true form" not even the past, because we are still in the process of seeing. But suddenly from outside the chamber, the Fox and Orual hear shouts that Psyche is coming with the gift of beauty. It is no longer a living image on a wall, but Psyche herself.

The Fox leads Orual out of the chamber, what had moments before been a judgment seat, a dark cavern, then an honest account of her life. They stand outside in the grassy courtyard before a pool of water with a mountain sky above. Yes, a mountain. Yes, that God of the mountain. And Psyche comes, and Orual falls at her feet, wholeheartedly repenting for her selfishness— "Never again will I call you mine; but all there is of me shall be yours" (305). Psyche draws her up and reminds her that she has not given the gift of beauty to Ungit yet. Yes, we remember. Orual is Ungit, has become her. As Psyche holds her hands, she burns Orual with the same touch of the immortal, the divine. She is radiant and "a thousand times more her very self" (306). Yes, the gift of beauty has been given. Orual is replete with joy, then she becomes aware of something greater. Was it a brighter light, a deeper color about her, a quaking within herself? Voices again announce. This time the god is coming. So much, so much Orual has come to understand. She is overwhelmed and already feels that she has been given all that she could ever desire as she and Psyche are reconciled forever.

Psyche brings Orual to the edge of the pool as the air itself grows brighter in the sunshine. The god's presence increases moment by moment, and Orual says that she feels as if she's being "unmade." He is coming, and everything exists for his sake. Orual knows this. No more questions, no more doubt, no more resistance. His presence is piercing her as she looks down. She sees herself in the pool, naked and unmade, next to clothed Psyche, yet they appear the same. <u>The god speaks and says to her</u>, not "You shall be," but "<u>You also are Psyche</u>" (308). She looks up to see him and wakes fully from the vision back in the palace gardens. The transformation is complete. The God of Love came just for her to complete what He promised. Orual is no longer ugly in any way but is wholly beautiful. His presence, His love is perfect and simple and transforming. Could this have been a baptism in the water's reflection? Possibly, but it seems more profound and final. The only water of death present has gone as the old washed away. Is anything left as a barrier between her and her God? No. Orual is at peace. Before her death a few days later, she confesses, "Before your face questions die away" (308), and Orual's life is brought to completion.

Conclusion

There is no fear in love. On the contrary, love that has achieved its goal gets rid of fear, because fear has to do with punishment; the person who keeps fearing has not been brought to maturity in regard to love. We ourselves love now because he loved us first.
—I John 4:18-19 (CJB)

COMING TO CHRIST is no panacea, but if C.S. Lewis were to tell us a tale of how pain and doubt were inevitable and unavoidable in a life of belief in God, who would willingly listen? It's one thing to share personal experience or to preach a lesson, but in fiction, an author and his audience might just be left with a moralizing and probably unlikeable character instead.

Most fiction features at least one appealing character—the one you cheer for, stumble with, return to. Therein lies one of the trickiest elements in *Till We Have Faces*. Perhaps one of the most exasperating characters of all of Lewis's novels, Orual is an unlikely blend for a central character. At the beginning of the tale, she is practically an orphaned girl without love or looks, and so we naturally pity her. By the time Psyche is born, it seems that Orual now has a purpose in life. In spite of her abusive father, she can now care for Psyche and be loved in return by Psyche and the Fox. Yet that same thing that brings joy to Orual also brings the most pain, and we begin to dislike Orual as she denies the truth of Psyche's sincere faith and even the god who revealed himself to her. Orual's long-term obstinacy and manipulation is offensive to us. We are frustrated by her resistance.

But there are moments of hope. When she ascends the mountain with Bardia, her heart delights in the beauty that surrounds her. In spite of the errand of grief, her heart is responsive. This is not just a sensitivity to nature, but a means by which God can speak to her. As her audience, we too hope that she might know God. Hope might also spur her to pray and ask the gods for their help after her first visit to the Grey Mountain. Yet Orual hears and feels nothing after hours of prayer. When we look at her in those moments, we can see that she is likely manipulating her religion. Orual wants things her own way because she only understands how to do things, to make things happen, in order to get something else. Her prayers are based on herself, not a sincere relationship with God. She selfishly demands an answer, and it must come in the way she chooses. Orual's wrestling is paralleled in James 1:6-8 (ESV): *But let him ask in faith, with no doubting, for the one who doubts is like a wave of the sea that is driven and tossed by the wind. For that person must not suppose that he will receive anything from the Lord; he is a double-minded man, unstable in all his ways.* Doubt is a harsh teacher, and it's probably because it stems from our own selfishness. With doubt in the way, Orual cannot see or hear the gods.

As most of us do then, if we cannot hear God, we blame Him. Orual declares, "The gods never send us this invitation to delight so readily or so strongly as when they are preparing some new agony. We are their bubbles; they blow us big before they prick us" (97). This same fatalism is echoed in James 1:13-15 (ESV): *Let no one say when he is tempted, 'I am being tempted by God,' for God cannot be tempted with evil, and he himself tempts no one. But each person is tempted when he is lured and enticed by his own desire. Then desire when it has conceived gives birth to sin, and sin when it is fully grown brings forth death.* Not one of us is helped by blaming God. Orual's domineering selfishness is key, and Ansit seems to be the only one to recognize it fully: "You're full fed. Gorged with other men's lives, women's too: Bardia's, mine the Fox's, your sister's—both your sisters'" (266). Orual is angered and repulsed by this, but she can see it is true. Whether her obsessive love for Psyche or her controlling love for Bardia, Orual's idea of love is wholly tainted. It brings death to all.

And so, how can we like a character who has damaged so many, including herself? This is the distinctive point of Lewis's tale. We don't have to like Orual or agree with her or even hope for her, but we do need to see ourselves in her. If we read this myth as story only, then we have lost its moral lesson and the pending redemption.

At the end of her reign, Orual finally realizes the futility of hiding from herself, "I did and I did and I did, and what does it matter that I did?" (236). She simply has no concept of what trust nor rest is. She has struggled with this from the beginning. Just as Psyche exemplifies complete, even perfect faith, Orual cannot trust. On her first visit to the mountain, Orual declares she almost came to a full belief (120). The almost is conscious doubt. She knows Psyche is certain, and she knows she, Orual, is not. It is a sickening feeling, and Orual is filled with both horror and grief at the gulf between them, immediately blaming the gods, instead of herself. She cannot see that she has in fact made a choice to doubt.

Moreover, when Orual returns to the mountain the second time determined to forcibly remove Psyche, she cannot see Psyche's perspective nor can she truly see Psyche's joy. Though Orual is certain she is right, she is blind. I John 2:8-11 says this is *because the darkness is passing away and the true light is already shining. Whoever says he is in the light and hates his brother is still in darkness. Whoever loves his brother abides in the light, and in him there is no cause for stumbling. But whoever hates his brother is in the darkness and walks in the darkness, and does not know where he is going, because the darkness has blinded his eyes.* Here, John reveals what Orual cannot know of herself yet—that she "hates" Psyche. This hatred incites her blindness, and by novel's end, Orual herself confesses to Psyche that she has always been a "craver," loving her only "selflessly" (305).

As Part II begins, Orual tells us that the gods began their

surgery and reopened her wounds. Her blindness cannot remain. Though it is an image of pain, it's also an image of rescue. The gods (God) will not allow her to hide behind the guise of "Queen." All of Orual must be seen. Ansit is the first to recognize that Orual both loves and devours just as Ungit does in the Great Sacrifice (265). Within Orual's dream and journey deep into the earth without her veil, Orual comes to understand who she is, the very thing she has never understood—Ungit. Before the dream, Arnom has just told Orual that Ungit was "the earth, the womb and mother of all living things" (270). And here Orual is, deep within the earth, seeing the reflection of Ungit in the mirror. Ungit is symbolic of our own ugliness, our selfishness, our sinfulness, not just Orual's. Though she wakes immediately, Orual's first reaction is to try to kill herself because she knows she cannot "fix" her ugliness. Little does she know that her rescue has begun.

In the midst of her final dream, Orual is answered by the gods, for now she knows without riddle they have always been there. Once Psyche gives her the gift of beauty and the God of the mountain appears and speaks to her, her ugliness is washed away. Orual had not been able to see until the end that love, real love, reveals truth incessantly, so that we can be like God. Yes, it takes all of Orual's life to come to this point, and even then, it is in a dream, yet now she can love herself and be loved by God fully. I John 3:2 says, *Beloved, we are God's children now, and what we will be has not yet appeared; but we know that when he appears we shall be like him, because we shall see him as he is.*

About the Author

CHRISTINE NORVELL is an author, speaker, and longtime educator. She graduated from Faulkner University with a Masters in Humanities and teaches high school literature and humanities at a classical Christian school.

She began playing the cello at age 11 and performed with the Tulsa Signature Symphony for over twenty years. Her own love of literature arose from summer reading programs and some inspiring classroom teachers.

As a speaker, Christine brings an appreciation for a variety of biblical and classical literary themes with an aim to help audiences probe deeper into writings and their own hearts. Speaking topics include Daily Bread: A Picture of God's Bakery; Why Pagan Literature; Teaching Nonfiction; Willa Cather and the Living Land; and The Tool of Story and God's Giftings.

Christine lives in Tulsa, Oklahoma, with her husband and three sons. She recommends Zion National Park and the Great Smokies for refreshing leisure. For updates on future books, lesson plans, and resources, subscribe to Christine's newsletter: www.thylyre.com, or follow her on www.facebook.com/thylyre and Twitter @thylyre.

Made in the USA
Lexington, KY
07 June 2017